The First Book of WordPerfect® for Windows™

Kate Miller

alpha books
A Division of Prentice Hall Computer Publishing
201 W. 103rd Street, Indianapolis, Indiana 46290 USA

International Standard Book Number: 1-56761-132-X
Library of Congress Catalog Card Number: 92-75143

96 95 94 93   8 7 6 5 4 3 2 1

Interpretation of the printing code: the rightmost number of the first series of numbers is the year of the book's printing; the rightmost number of the second series of numbers is the number of the book's printing. For example, a printing code of 93-1 shows that the first printing of the book occurred in 1993.

Printed in the United States of America

Publisher
Marie Butler-Knight

Associate Publisher
Lisa Bucki

Managing Editor
Elizabeth Keaffaber

Acquisitions Manager
Stephen R. Poland

Development Editor
Faithe Wempen

Production Editor
Michelle Shaw

Copy Editor
Barry Childs-Helton

Cover Artist
Susan Kniola

Indexer
Jeanne Clark

Production Team
Diana Bigham, Katy Bodenmiller,
Ayrika Bryant, Brad Chinn,
Scott Cook, Tim Cox, Meshell
Dinn, Mark Enochs, Howard
Jones, Carrie Roth, Greg Simsic

*Special thanks to Avon Murphy
for ensuring the technical accuracy of this book.*

Contents

Introduction

The *First Book of WordPerfect 6, Bestseller Edition* helped almost 100,000 people learn WordPerfect quickly. Now, the edition has been updated for WordPerfect's exciting 6.0 for Windows version, and improved to provide even more help.

Popular word processors usually have hundreds of features for you to learn to use. This is more than the average user needs or wants, and for the beginning user, the sheer bulk can be intimidating. What *The First Book of WordPerfect 6.0 for Windows* does is glean only the most-used features. It focuses on those features you'll need to use in the great majority of your work. This way, you save time and eliminate the frustration of trying to sort out what you need from what you don't need.

Conventions Used in This Book

Read "In This Chapter" at the beginning of each chapter for a brief idea of what you'll learn in the chapter. The most important procedures are summarized at the beginning of every chapter, too, so if you're in a hurry, you don't need to wade through any text to find what you need. Throughout the chapter, tables, notes, tips, cautions, FYI Ideas, and steps make learning easy.

Once you have learned WordPerfect for Windows, you may need an occasional reminder. The tear-out Quick Reference Card summarizes WordPerfect commands you may encounter most often—in handy, take-along form.

Several special icons are used in this book:

QUICK STEPS

The generous number of Quick Steps give you the at-a-glance steps you need to perform an operation quickly. These numbered steps describe both the actions you perform, and the results of those actions. The inside front cover provides a list of Quick Steps for fast reference.

TIP: These provide hints and shortcuts for using the program more effectively.

NOTE: These show additional features, and provide the background information you need to understand special terms.

CAUTION

These alert you to potential pitfalls, and help solve common problems.

FYI IDEAS

These describe practical ways you can use WordPerfect at work and at home to create projects and documents you may not have imagined.

Entering Commands

WordPerfect allows you to select commands with the mouse or keypresses. The instructions in this book cover both options. Work with whatever approach is most comfortable for you. Keystrokes to be made in combination are separated by a plus (+), and in this book, are represented by small keycap illustrations meant to resemble your computer's keys. For example, Ctrl+Q indicates you should press **Ctrl** and **Q** simultaneously.

When an operation is described as follows:

Press F9, or choose Font from the Layout menu.

it means there are two different methods of accomplishing the same thing. The first method would be to press the F9 key. The second method would be to pull down the Layout menu (you'll learn how to do this later in the book), and select the Font option from it. (The bold letter in the command indicates that you can choose it by typing that letter.)

Acknowledgments

Many thanks for the continued excellent support from the staff at Prentice Hall Computer Publishing. Special thanks to Marie Butler-Knight, Liz Keaffaber, Faithe Wempen, Michelle Shaw, and Barry Childs-Helton.

Trademark Acknowledgments

All terms mentioned in this book that are known to be trademarks or service marks are listed below. In addition, terms suspected of being trademarks or service marks have been appropriately capitalized. Alpha Books cannot attest to the accuracy of this information. Use of a term in this book should not be regarded as affecting the validity of any trademark or service mark.

CorelDRAW! is a registered trademark of Corel Systems Corporation.

MS-DOS, Excel, MS Word, and Windows are registered trademarks of Microsoft Corporation.

Ami Pro and Lotus 1-2-3 are registered trademarks of Lotus Development Corporation.

Quattro Pro is a registered trademark of Borland International.

Starting Windows

1. At the DOS prompt, type WIN and press ↵Enter.

Mouse Use

- Point: To move the mouse until the pointer on-screen points to a specified item.
- Click: To press and release the left mouse button.
- Double-click: To press and release the left mouse button twice in a row quickly.
- Drag: To hold down the left mouse button while you move the mouse.

Quitting Windows

1. Open the File menu.
2. Select Exit Windows.
3. If asked to confirm, select OK.

A Quick Overview of Windows

If you're not sure how to get started, here's some help. If you are a newcomer to computers (or want to review the basics), take a look at Appendix A, "The Basics for Beginners." If you have fundamental knowledge of computers and word processing, but are unfamiliar with using Windows, start with this chapter. If you are handy with Windows, move ahead to Chapter 2, "Getting Started with WordPerfect for Windows."

To use WordPerfect 6.0 for Windows effectively, you must first understand the Windows environment. *Windows* is a framework that allows you to use your computer more easily, and use more than one application at a time. Windows does not replace sophisticated word processors or spreadsheets. Instead, Windows provides a *graphical* (picture-oriented) environment for using applications alone or together. Windows is aptly named. You will be able to move between applications (and documents within applications) via graphic rectangles called *windows*. Every window has a name so you can identify it, and moving from window to window is easy.

Windows makes learning to use your computer easier. And, once you understand the conventions used in Windows, you can master *Windows applications* (programs such as WordPerfect for Windows) quickly. Windows also enables you to move information easily between applications. For example, you can use WordPerfect for Windows as your word processor, and Lotus 1-2-3 to build spreadsheets. With Windows, you can transfer data easily from your spreadsheet to your WordPerfect document. This transfer can occur whether or not the application was built to run under Windows. (For more details, see Chapter 18, "Getting Information From and To Other Sources.")

Starting Windows

Starting Windows is easy. Just type **WIN** and press `⏎Enter`. If you installed Windows on a different drive, an extra step is involved: type in the letter of the drive where Windows is installed, followed by a colon (such as **D:**) and press `⏎Enter`. Then type **WIN** and press `⏎Enter`.

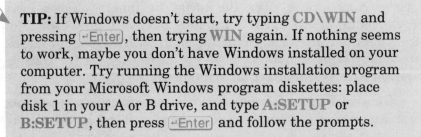

TIP: If Windows doesn't start, try typing **CD\WIN** and pressing `⏎Enter`, then trying **WIN** again. If nothing seems to work, maybe you don't have Windows installed on your computer. Try running the Windows installation program from your Microsoft Windows program diskettes: place disk 1 in your A or B drive, and type **A:SETUP** or **B:SETUP**, then press `⏎Enter` and follow the prompts.

A screen with the version number of Windows appears briefly, followed by the Windows Program Manager screen.

A Windows Screen

Master one screen in Windows, and you've mastered them all. Each screen in Windows (or in a Windows application) is designed

with the same basic components. WordPerfect for Windows is no
exception. Figure 1.1 shows a typical screen in Windows, followed
by a list that describes its components. (Ways to manipulate the
screen components with the mouse and keyboard are covered later
in this chapter.)

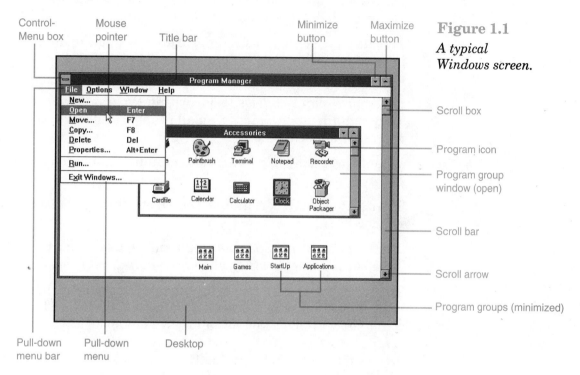

Figure 1.1

A typical Windows screen.

The *mouse pointer*: If you have a mouse installed, the
mouse pointer (a small arrow) shows where your next
mouse action will take effect. For example, if the mouse
pointer is pointing to a command on a menu, clicking the
mouse button will select that command.

The *Title bar* shows the name of the application or the
document. The title of the active window (the one currently available for use) is in a different color or intensity.
In Figure 1.2, the application running is Program Manager.

The *Maximize button* is used to enlarge an application window to occupy the entire screen. It may also be used to enlarge an application document to occupy the entire application workspace.

Once a window is maximized, you may use the *Restore button* to shrink the window to its previous size.

The *Minimize button* is used to shrink a window to an icon, which clears the desktop of an application or document not currently in use.

Program Group Windows reside within Program Manager. They contain *program icons*, small graphic symbols that represent applications.

When a program group window is minimized, it becomes a *Program group icon.*

The *desktop* is the background screen on which you display windows.

The *Pull-down menu bar*, located immediately under the Title bar of an application, shows the *pull-down menus.*

The *scroll bar* is used to display parts of a document that don't appear on-screen when a document is too long. The *scroll box* within a scroll bar allows you to make large jumps from one point in a document to another. *Scroll arrows* move you more gradually.

The *Control Menu box* is used to open the Control Menu, which allows you to change the size of a window, move the window around on the desktop, and exit (close) a window or application when you are done using it.

Using a Mouse

If you have never used a mouse before, some of the terminology used in this book may seem strange to you. Here's a quick summary of the mouse techniques you need to know.

- **Point:** To move the mouse until the pointer on-screen points to a specified item.

- **Click:** To press and release the left mouse button.

- **Double-click:** To press and release the left mouse button twice in a row quickly.

- **Drag:** To hold down the left mouse button while you move the mouse.

Practice these techniques in Windows until you become familiar with them; if you use a mouse with WordPerfect for Windows, these skills will be very important. Figure 1.2 shows how to use the mouse to perform common Windows activities, including running applications and moving and resizing windows.

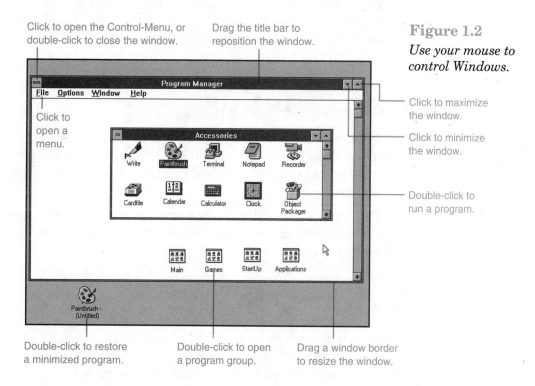

Figure 1.2

Use your mouse to control Windows.

Starting a Program

To start a program, simply double-click on its icon or highlight it and press ⏎Enter. If its icon is contained in a program group window that's not open at the moment, open the window first. Follow these steps:

1. If necessary, open the program group window that contains the program you want to run. To open a program group window, double-click on its icon. For example, to open the WordPerfect for Windows program group, double-click on the program group icon that says WordPerfect for Windows under it.

2. Double-click on the icon for the program you want to run. For example, to run WordPerfect for Windows, click on the WordPerfect for Windows icon (the one in the WordPerfect for Windows program group that looks like a pen).

Using Menus

The pull-down menu bar (see Figure 1.3) contains various menus from which you can select commands. Each Windows program that you run has a set of pull-down menus; Windows itself has a set too.

To open a menu, click on its name on the menu bar. Once a menu is open, you can select a command from it by clicking on the desired command.

Accelerator keys. Notice that in Figure 1.3, some commands are followed by key names such as Enter (for the **O**pen command) or F8 (for the **C**opy command). These are called *accelerator keys*. You can use these keys to perform these commands without even opening the menu.

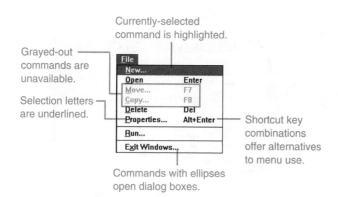

Grayed-out commands are unavailable.

Currently-selected command is highlighted.

Selection letters are underlined.

Shortcut key combinations offer alternatives to menu use.

Commands with ellipses open dialog boxes.

Figure 1.3

A menu lists various commands you can perform.

Usually, when you select a command, the command is performed immediately. However:

- If the command name is gray (rather than black), the command is unavailable at the moment and you cannot choose it.

- If the command name is followed by an arrow, selecting the command will cause another menu to appear, from which you select another command.

- If the command name is followed by ellipses (three dots), selecting it will cause a dialog box to appear. You'll learn about dialog boxes in the next section.

Navigating Dialog Boxes

A *dialog box* is Windows' way of requesting additional information. For example, if you choose **P**rint from the **F**ile menu within the Windows accessory called Write, you'll see the dialog box shown in Figure 1.4.

Figure 1.4
*A typical
dialog box.*

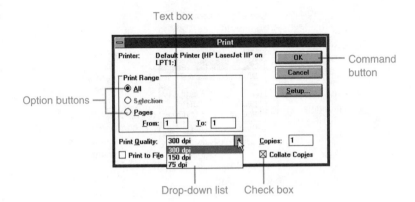

Each dialog box contains one or more of the following elements:

- *List boxes* display available choices. To activate a list, click inside the list box. If the entire list is not visible, use the scroll bar to view the items in the list. To select an item from the list, click on it.

- *Drop-down lists* are similar to list boxes, but only one item in the list is shown. To see the rest of the items, click on the down arrow to the right of the list box. To select an item from the list, click on it.

- *Text boxes* allow you to type an entry. To activate a text box, click inside it. To edit an existing entry, use the arrow keys to move the cursor, and the Del or Backspace keys to delete existing characters, and then type your correction.

- *Check boxes* allow you to select one or more items in a group of options. For example, if you are styling text, you may select Bold and Italic to have the text appear in both bold and italic type. Click on a check box to activate it.

- *Option buttons* are like check boxes, but you can select only one option button in a group. Selecting one button unselects any option that is already selected. Click on an option button to activate it.

- *Command buttons* execute (or cancel) the command once you have made your selections in the dialog box. To press a command button, click on it.

Switching Between Windows

Many times you will have more than one window open at once. Some open windows may be program group windows, while others may be actual programs that are running. To switch among them, you can:

- Pull down the Window menu and choose the window you want to view; or

- If a portion of the desired window is visible, click on it.

Controlling a Window

A window at maximum size occupies the entire screen. When a window is maximized, you may click on the Restore button to restore the window to its original size. When a window is minimized, it becomes an icon. You may double-click on the icon, or use the Restore command (or button) to restore the icon to a full-size window.

To maximize or minimize a window with the mouse:

- Click on the Maximize (up arrow) or Minimize (down arrow) buttons in the upper right corner of the window you want to resize. If a window is maximized, click on the Restore button (up-and-down arrow) to restore it to its original size.

To maximize or minimize a window with the keyboard:

1. Make sure the window is active.

2. Access the Control-Menu (use Alt+Spacebar for an application window or dialog box, and use Alt+- for a document window).

3. To switch between a full-screen window (the maximum) and an icon (the minimum), select Minimize, Maximize, or Restore from the Control-Menu.

Closing a Window

To exit or close an active window, use either the mouse or the keyboard with the Control-Menu.

To close a window with the mouse:

- Double-click on the Control-Menu box in the upper left corner of the screen.

To close a window with the keyboard:

- Select the Control-Menu box (press Alt+Spacebar for the active application window or dialog box, and Alt+ - for the active document window). Now select Close.

    or

- Select the window you wish to close, and press Alt+F4 (the shortcut key for closing an active window).

Copying Your Program Diskettes

Before you install any new software, you should make a copy of the original diskettes as a safety precaution. Windows' File Manager makes this process easy.

First, start File Manager by double-clicking on the File Manager icon in the Main program group. Then, for each disk you need to copy, follow these steps:

1. Locate a blank disk of the same type as the original disk, and label it to match the original. Make sure the disk you select does not contain any data that you want to keep.

2. Place the original disk in your diskette drive (A or B).

3. Open the Disk menu and select Copy Disk. The Copy Disk dialog box appears.

4. Select the drive used in step 2 from the **S**ource In list box.

5. Select the same drive from the **D**estination In list box. (Don't worry; File Manager will tell you to switch disks at the appropriate time.)

6. Select OK. The Confirm Copy Disk dialog box appears.

7. Select Yes to continue.

8. When instructed to insert the Source diskette, choose OK, since you already did this at step 2. The Copying Disk box appears, and the copy process begins.

9. When instructed to insert the target disk, remove the original disk from the drive and insert the blank disk. Then choose OK to continue. The Copying Disk box disappears when the process is complete.

Quitting Windows

Before you quit Windows, always save the files you have created or updated, and close each application. If the active application is designed to work with Windows, select the Exit Windows command from the File menu. If the application is not designed to work with Windows, use the exit procedure specified for that application, and exit Windows separately afterward.

Once all applications are closed, you may quit Windows from the Program Manager screen. Select File, then Exit Windows. The Exit Windows dialog box appears with the Save Changes option checked. (When **S**ave Changes is checked, any changes you have made to the Program Manager settings will be saved and used the next time you start up Windows.) From the Exit Windows dialog box, select OK to quit windows or Cancel to continue working in Windows.

Starting WordPerfect

1. Type win at the DOS prompt and press ⏎Enter.
2. Double-click on the WPWin 6.0 program group icon, or press Ctrl+Tab⇆ to highlight its icon and press ⏎Enter.
3. Double-click on the WPWin 6.0 program icon, or use the arrow keys to highlight it and then press ⏎Enter.

Selecting a Command from a Pull-Down Menu

1. Click on the menu name, or press Alt and type the menu name's selection letter.
2. Click on the command, or type the selection letter of the command name.

Getting Help

1. Select Help from the menu bar, or press F1.

Ways to Exit WordPerfect

- Select Exit from the File menu.
- Press Alt+F4.

2

Getting Started with WordPerfect 6.0 for Windows

Welcome to the quick and easy way to learn WordPerfect for Windows. If you're not sure how to get started, this chapter will provide some help. In it, you'll learn how to start WordPerfect for Windows, how to move around and enter commands, and how to use the on-line Help feature.

TIP: If you're a newcomer to computers (or want to review the basics), take a look at Appendix A, "Getting Ready to Use WordPerfect for Windows."

Starting WordPerfect for Windows

Once WordPerfect for Windows is installed, you are ready to begin using the program. If WordPerfect for Windows has not been installed on your computer, refer to Appendix B, "Installing WordPerfect for Windows" for instructions. When you're ready, follow these steps.

1. Make sure the computer is turned on.

2. Start Windows (usually by typing `win` at the DOS prompt; see Chapter 1 for more information).

3. On the Windows Program Manager screen, you will see the WordPerfect *program group icon* shown in Figure 2.1. Or, if the program group is already open, you'll see the WPWin 6.0 *program group window* shown in Figure 2.2.

Figure 2.1

The WordPerfect Program Group icon.

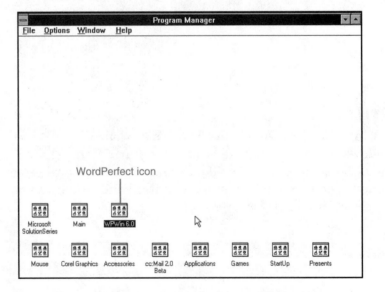

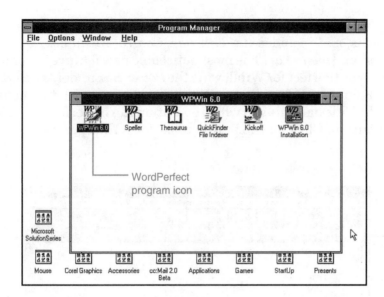

Figure 2.2
*The WPWin 6.0
program group
window.*

4. If what you see looks like Figure 2.1, select the WPWin 6.0 program group icon by double-clicking on it with the mouse, or by pressing Ctrl + Tab ↹ to highlight the icon, and then pressing ↵Enter. The WPWin 6.0 program group opens, as shown in Figure 2.2.

5. In the WPWin 6.0 program group, double-click on the WPWin 6.0 program icon, or use the arrow keys to highlight it and then press ↵Enter. WordPerfect for Windows starts.

When you finish these steps, WordPerfect for Windows should appear on your screen.

The WordPerfect Document Window

The first thing you'll see when you start WordPerfect for Windows is a document window like the one in Figure 2.3.

Notice that the screen layout follows typical Windows conventions, and includes the *Title bar*, *Control-Menu box*, *window border*, and *menu bar*. The most noticeable new feature in version 6.0 of WordPerfect for Windows is the *Power Bar* under the *Button Bar*. Point at a Power Bar or Button Bar button with the mouse, and the Title bar tells you which operation can be performed using that button. Click on the button to perform the operation.

Figure 2.3
The WordPerfect document window.

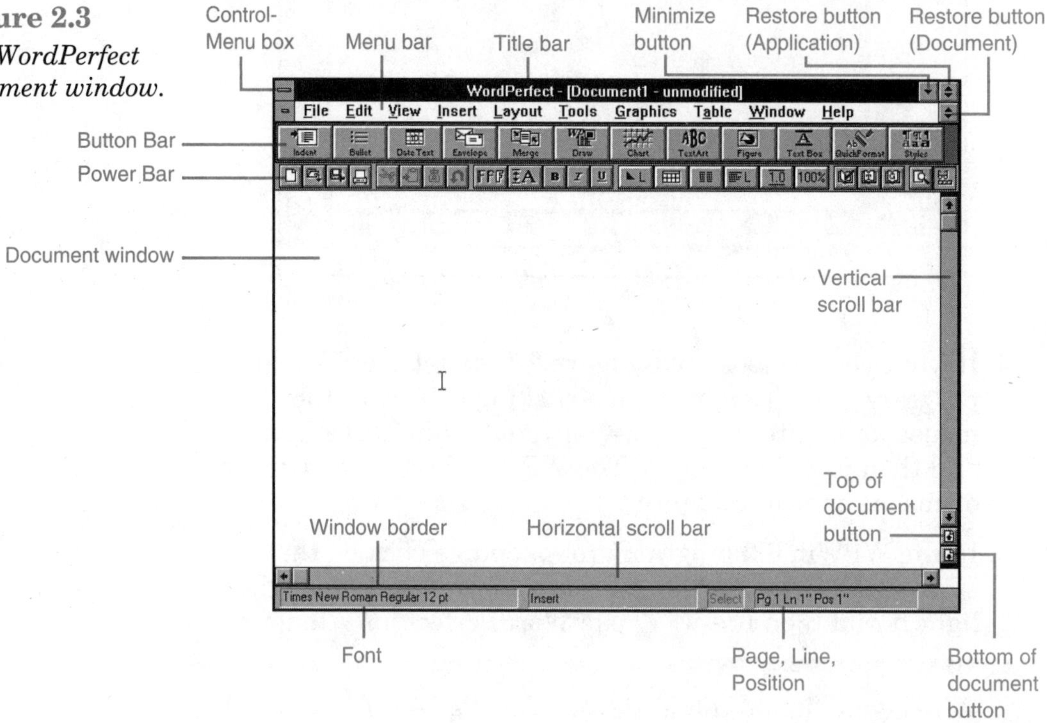

Scroll bars allow you to use the mouse to move rapidly through a document. The buttons below the vertical scroll bar allow you to move quickly to the top or bottom of a document.

Also available on the WordPerfect document window are the *Minimize* and *Restore buttons* for the WordPerfect for Windows application, as well as a Restore button for the document window. In addition to standard Windows features, the current font appears in the lower left corner; the lower right corner shows the page number, line number, and insertion point position within the window.

Making WordPerfect Selections

When you work with WordPerfect, usually you have three options for selecting WordPerfect functions. You can:

- Make a menu selection from the menu bar (with the keyboard or mouse).

- Use a *shortcut key*. Just press a function key, alone or in combination with the Alt, ⇧Shift, or Ctrl keys. The function keys are labeled F1 through F10 or F12. Each combination is assigned a special use in WordPerfect for Windows.

- Click on a button on the Power Bar or Button Bar.

Because the menu bar provides an easy way for a beginner to access commands without memorizing function keys, we'll start our discussion there.

WordPerfect Menus

A *menu* on a computer screen is similar to a menu in a restaurant. For example, in a restaurant you might select a steak from the menu, and then be asked how you want it cooked, what side dishes you want, and what kind of dressing you want on your salad. Likewise, in WordPerfect, each menu offers several selections, and once you make a choice, you are often asked to make additional decisions about how you want the command to execute.

For example, Figure 2.3 shows the menu bar. If you select File, the options for handling a file appear. The File menu is shown in Figure 2.4. The menus that appear from the menu bar are often referred to as *pull-down menus*, since they appear to be pulled down from the menu bar. Notice that from the File menu, you can print, exit WordPerfect, or select any other option related to file handling.

Each of the menu bar items has a different colored, bold, or underlined letter, indicating what letter you would type to select it. These are called *selection letters*. When you open a menu, you'll see that each item on the menu has a selection letter, too. You'll see how these selection letters come in handy in the next section.

Figure 2.4
The File menu (a pull-down menu).

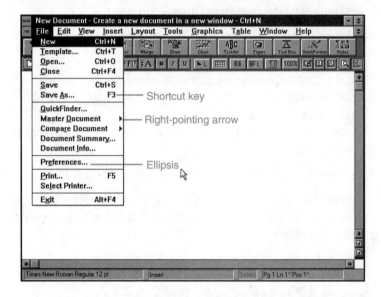

To use WordPerfect's pull-down menus, you activate the menu bar, select a pull-down menu, and then select a command from the menu. Depending on the command you select, it will either open a *cascading menu*, open a *dialog box*, or execute immediately.

You can tell by looking at a menu command what will happen when you select it (see Figure 2.4). Menu commands with right-pointing arrows to their right will open additional menus called *cascading menus*. Commands followed by ellipses open *dialog boxes*. A dialog box is a special window that prompts you to perform a specific operation when it appears. Commands with neither of these things beside them execute immediately.

Some commands may not be available at all times. For example, you cannot access the **P**aste command until you have used **C**ut or **C**opy to mark something to be pasted. Options that are temporarily unavailable appear in lighter (*grayed-out*) text. (There aren't any grayed-out commands shown in Figure 2.4; all **F**ile menu commands are available.)

Getting Started

Most of the menu commands have *shortcut key equivalents*, such as pressing  F3 to save and name a file. The shortcut keys are listed on the pull-down menus next to the command names (see Figure 2.4). Users who are already familiar with a previous version of WordPerfect may prefer the shortcut keys to using the menus.

However, the menu bar is the best tool for beginners. Menu actions are grouped on the menus logically. If you are unsure of the keys to press to perform a function, browse through the menus. Even sophisticated word processing users will hunt for commands as they become familiar with a new word processing system. Then, once you are more familiar with WordPerfect, you may want to begin using the key combinations to speed up your work.

Choosing Commands from Menus

You can use either the keyboard or a mouse to choose a command from the menu bar. Experiment with both methods to see which you prefer. Follow these Quick Steps to select a menu command with the mouse.

Choosing a Menu Command with a Mouse

1. Move the mouse on your desk until the pointer is over the menu name you want.

   The mouse pointer appears as a small arrow on your screen.

2. Click the left mouse button to pull down the menu.

   The menu appears. For example, if you clicked on File, the File menu would appear, as shown in Figure 2.4.

3. To make menu selections, point at the item and click the left mouse button.

   The command is executed, or WordPerfect opens another menu or dialog box to request more information.

4. If prompted, provide additional information in the dialog box that appears, or click on a command from the cascading menu that appears.

If you open a menu and then decide you want to escape from it without selecting any command, just click the mouse anywhere outside the menu.

The following Quick Steps show how to choose a menu command with the keyboard.

Choosing a Menu Command with the Keyboard

1. Press Alt.

The Control Menu box next to the menu bar is highlighted.

2. Type the selection letter (the bold, underlined, or highlighted letter) in the desired menu name. For example, type **F** for the **F**ile menu.

The selected pull-down menu appears. Each command on the pull-down menu has a selection letter.

3. Type the selection letter for the command you want to select.

The command is executed, or WordPerfect opens another menu or dialog box to request more information.

4. If prompted, provide additional information in the dialog box that appears, or choose a command from the cascading menu that appears.

TIP: You can press Alt and the selection letter simultaneously, combining steps 1 and 2 to make the procedure quicker.

If you get into a menu or dialog box and then decide you want to exit from it without selecting a command, just press Esc until you're back to the regular editing screen.

Special Markings on Menus

You may have already encountered some of WordPerfect's special markings on menus that help you get around, such as an ellipsis (...) after a command. Here's a quick rundown of the marks.

Right-pointing arrows indicate that the command opens a smaller menu called a *cascading menu*. For example, the Master **D**ocument command on the **F**ile menu opens a cascading menu (see Figure 2.5). You select commands from a cascading menu exactly as you do regular menu commands: either click on them or type their selection letter.

Figure 2.5

The File Master Document cascading menu.

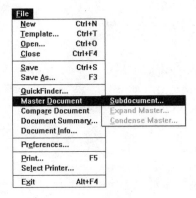

Another visual prompt on a menu is a *check* before the command. When you see one, it means the command is selected. For example, in Figure 2.6, the **V**iew menu has the **P**age Mode, **B**utton Bar, **P**ower Bar, St**a**tus Bar, and **G**raphics options marked.

An *ellipsis (...)* after a command indicates that a dialog box or window will appear, allowing you to check or change option settings or type in information to complete the command. See "Dialog Boxes," later in this chapter, for more information.

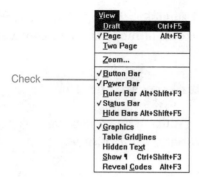

Check ─────

Figure 2.6
Menu commands selected.

Using Shortcut Keys

Shortcut keys circumvent the sometimes-lengthy route through several menus to a particular feature. For example, to leave WordPerfect for Windows, you can select the File menu and then select Exit, or you can simply use the keyboard shortcut Alt + F4.

NOTE: Shortcut keys primarily involve function keys (the F keys: F1, F2, and so on). Occasionally, other keys are used, such as Ctrl + S to save a document.

When using a shortcut key, you might press a function key alone, or in conjunction with one or more other keys (usually some combination of Ctrl, Shift, or Alt). To use a key combination (such as Alt + F4), just hold down the keys simultaneously. If you find that difficult, hold down the first key while pressing the second.

The Keyboard

The quickest way to perform an operation or command is with a shortcut key combination. Each function key executes a separate operation by itself, with the ⌂Shift key, with the Ctrl key, and with the Alt key—for a total of more than 40 commands.

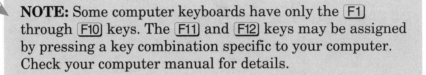

NOTE: Some computer keyboards have only the F1 through F10 keys. The F11 and F12 keys may be assigned by pressing a key combination specific to your computer. Check your computer manual for details.

Don't be intimidated by the number of key options on the template. Use this book to get started, and you will learn the most useful functions first. Concentrate on learning key combinations for the functions you use most. The more you use them, the more the key combinations will become second nature to you.

Moving the Insertion Point

The *insertion point* locates the position for any text you type. You can move it around the screen, and use it to designate where you want certain commands to take effect. By default, it appears as a blinking vertical line.

CAUTION   Don't confuse the insertion point with the *mouse pointer*. (You can move the insertion point by using the mouse, however, as you'll learn later.) The insertion point is a plain vertical line; the mouse pointer takes various shapes, including an arrow, an I-beam (looks like a curly capital I), and an hourglass.

Insertion Point Movement with the Keyboard

Some keyboard actions enable you to move the insertion point quickly. These are called *quick movement keys*. Table 2.1 summarizes the quick movement keys. You will probably want to refer to this table frequently as you begin working in WordPerfect.

Move	Keys to Press
One character left	`←`
One character right	`→`
Left a word	`Ctrl` with `←` (Word Left)
Right a word	`Ctrl` with `→` (Word Right)
Up a single line	`↑`
Down a single line	`↓`
Move to top of screen (then up a screen)	`PgUp`
First line of previous page	`Alt`+`PgUp`
First line of next page	`Alt`+`PgDn`
Move to bottom of screen (then down a screen)	`PgDn`
Up a paragraph	`Ctrl`+`↑`
Down a paragraph	`Ctrl`+`↓`
Beginning of document (after WordPerfect codes)	`Ctrl`+`Home`
Beginning of document (before WordPerfect codes)	`Ctrl`+`Home`, `Ctrl`+`Home`
End of document (after WordPerfect codes)	`Ctrl`+`End`
Beginning of page	`Alt`+`Home`
End of page	`Alt`+`End`
Go to a page number you type in	`Ctrl`+`G`
Left end of line, before codes	`Home`, `Home`
Left end of line, after codes	`Home`
Right end of line, after codes	`End`

Table 2.1
Quick Movement Keys

Working with Dialog Boxes

Dialog boxes are special windows that appear to perform specific operations. Dialog boxes allow you to enter required information or select from options.

Selection and movement in dialog boxes are a little different from the same procedures in menus. Figures 2.7 and 2.8 illustrate the common methods of supplying information in dialog boxes. Don't worry about what the boxes shown here do; just look at the various ways they provide for you to make decisions.

To move around a dialog box with the keyboard, use the Tab ↕ key to move forward or ⇧Shift + Tab ↕ to move backward. Once you're in a section, use the arrow keys to select among the choices. Moving around with the mouse is easy; just click on the option you want.

Figure 2.7

The Print dialog box.

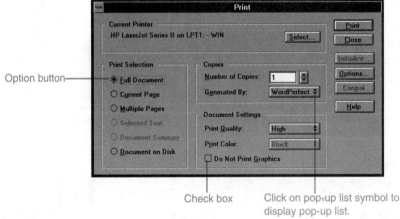

Option button

Check box

Click on pop-up list symbol to display pop-up list.

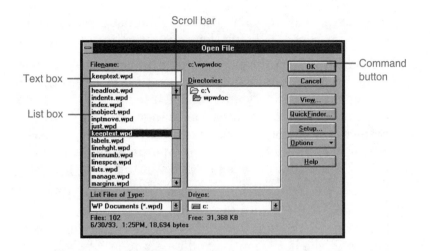

Figure 2.8
The Open File dialog box.

Check boxes: Check boxes are used for situations where a feature is either on or off. If the check box has an X in it, the option is on; if it doesn't, the option is off. Click on the check box (or press its selection letter) to change its status.

Option buttons: Option buttons are sometimes called *radio buttons* because—just like on a car radio—only one button can be selected at a time. When you press a second button, the first one pops back out. Option buttons are used for multiple-choice questions like *"Which of these four layouts do you want?"* Click on the option you want, or press its selection letter.

Lists: Lists allow you to select a single choice from a list. Sometimes, just like pull-down menus, the lists are hidden until you select the menu name. A double-headed arrow symbol indicates a hidden pop-up list. A downward pointing arrow indicates a pull-down list. Open these lists by clicking on the arrow, or by pressing Alt plus the selection letter and then Spacebar. Make a selection from the list by clicking on it or by using the arrow keys to highlight it.

Text boxes: Text boxes are used to type in information, such as a file name. If an arrow appears at the end of the text box, you can click on it to reveal a list from which to choose, or press ⟨Alt⟩ plus the selection letter and then ⟨↓⟩.

Command buttons: Command buttons are used to get away from the dialog box. For example, OK closes the dialog box, and puts your changes into effect. Cancel closes the dialog box, and ignores the changes you may have made to the dialog box settings. Other buttons, such as Setup in Figure 2.8, take you temporarily away from the dialog box without closing it. Click on them, or ⟨Tab↹⟩ to them and press ⟨↵Enter⟩.

List boxes: List boxes are used to select one item from a list. They're like pull-down lists, except they're always visible. If the list is long, scroll bars and/or arrow keys are used to move through it. In Figure 2.8, the item selected appears about halfway through the list.

Scroll Bars

You may have noticed in the list box in Figure 2.8 that a *scroll bar* appeared when there were more options than could be shown in the fixed area allotted for the list box. Scroll bars appear at the bottom and right sides of documents too if the documents are too large to be displayed on the screen all at once. They help mouse users move quickly through the list or document. You can't use the keyboard to control scroll bars.

To use a scroll bar follow these steps:

- Drag the box in the scroll bar to the approximate point in the list where you want to be. For example, drag the box to the bottom of the scroll bar to go quickly to the end of the list.

- Click on the arrows at the end of the scroll bar to move a line at a time.

- Click and hold on an arrow to move continuously.

- To move a screen up or down, click above or below the scroll box on the vertical scroll bar.

- If there is a horizontal scroll bar, you can move a screen right or left by clicking to the right or left of the scroll box on the bar.

The Power Bar

WordPerfect for Windows 6.0 comes with a *Power Bar* set up to provide quick access to commonly-used commands on each button. The Power Bar is one more option (besides the menus or pressing keys), you can use to select a few of the WordPerfect commands. If the Power Bar is not displayed, follow these steps to display it:

1. Open the View menu.

2. Select Power Bar.

When a check appears before Power Bar, it is displayed. Remove the check and the Power Bar disappears.

Point at a button with the mouse pointer to see a description of that button's use in the title bar. (You cannot use the keyboard to make a Power Bar selection.) If a button is not available, it appears grayed. This indicates that some operation needs to be completed before you can choose that button.

Displaying and Using the Power Bar

1. If the Power Bar is not displayed, select View Power Bar.	The Power Bar appears.
2. Click on a button.	The operation of the button is performed.
3. To deselect the Power Bar, select View Power Bar again.	The Power Bar disappears.

Table 2.1 shows the default buttons on the Power Bar and explains what they do.

Table 2.1
The Default Power Bar Buttons

Button	Purpose
	Begins a new document
	Open an existing document
	Saves the current document
	Prints the current document
	Cuts the selected text to the Clipboard
	Copies the selected text to the Clipboard
	Pastes the selected text from the Clipboard
	Reverses the last editing action
	Changes the font
	Changes the font size
	Turns on/off the bold attribute
	Turns on/off the italic attribute
	Turns on/off the underline attribute
	Sets tabs

Button	Purpose
	Creates tables
	Formats text in multiple columns
	Aligns (justifies) text
	Sets space between lines
	Controls magnification at which document is shown
	Checks spelling
	Opens thesaurus
	Checks grammar
	Shows the page full-size as it will print
	Turns on/off the Button Bar

The Button Bar

When installed, WordPerfect for Windows is set up with the Button Bar appearing. The Button Bar allows you to perform actions quickly with a click of the mouse. To control the display of the Button Bar, select View, then Button Bar. When **B**utton Bar is checked, the Button Bar appears.

To see a description of each button in the Button Bar, place the mouse pointer on the button. A description appears in the title bar. To choose a button, just click on it (buttons in the Button Bar cannot be selected using the keyboard). Also, buttons that are grayed cannot be selected, because some other operation must be performed first.

A major difference between the Button Bar and the Power Bar is that you can create and edit Button Bars to include activities you perform often. Chapter 20, "Button Bars and the Power Bar," describes more advanced options available for both.

Help!

WordPerfect can answer your cry of "Help!" Just select Help from the menu bar. The first three options on the pull-down menu allow you to choose:

- **Contents:** Select Contents to see the full contents of Help—Help's "main lobby."

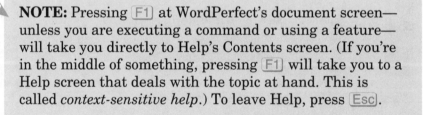

NOTE: Pressing F1 at WordPerfect's document screen—unless you are executing a command or using a feature—will take you directly to Help's Contents screen. (If you're in the middle of something, pressing F1 will take you to a Help screen that deals with the topic at hand. This is called *context-sensitive help*.) To leave Help, press Esc.

- **Search for Help On:** Select Search for Help On, and the same screen accessed through the **Help** Contents Search Index appears. You can choose from an alphabetical list of features. When you choose a feature, the keystrokes for using the feature appear, along with the steps and other referenced information.

- **How Do I:** Select How Do I to see a list of typical tasks to be performed in WordPerfect.

TIP: From within Help, you may double-click on an under-lined word to jump to a related topic. Don't worry about getting lost; you can always use the Back button to move back a topic.

- **Macros:** Select Macros to get special help about using *macros* (recorded sequences of keypresses which allow you to automate WordPerfect activities).

- **Coach:** Choose Coach, and you can select a task to receive prompting as you work. For example, if you can't remember how to create a table of contents, you can use a coach to walk you through the process.

- **Tutorial:** Choose Tutorial to work with your own private "teacher." The tutorial program has lessons about common activities, such as editing text and formatting text. You may also choose from a topic list.

Take some time to play with the Help feature. It can answer your questions and save you some frustrating moments.

NOTE: If you exhaust the help alternatives within your immediate control (including referring to the reference manuals provided), a call to WordPerfect Corporation's technical support group will usually clear up any lingering problems. Current phone numbers are listed in the WordPerfect Reference Manual. Before calling, prepare yourself. Be ready to provide a detailed description of the problem, and know the type of computer and version of WordPerfect you are using.

Exiting WordPerfect for Windows

It is important to exit WordPerfect for Windows properly. This will avoid damage to your documents or to WordPerfect programs. The following Quick Steps cover how to exit.

WordPerfect

1. Press Alt with F4, or select Exit from the File menu.

   If you have changes to one or more documents that have not been saved, the WordPerfect dialog box appears.

2. Identify whether you want to save changes to each document.

   Files are saved according to your instructions. Then you are returned to Windows.

TIP: You can also double-click on the Control-Menu box in the upper left corner of the WordPerfect window to exit.

Turning on Reveal Codes

1. Select Reveal Codes from the View menu, or press `Alt`+`F3`.
2. Repeat step 1 to remove the Reveal Codes screen.

Toggling Between Insert and Typeover Modes

1. Press `Ins` to toggle between Insert and Typeover modes.

Ways to Delete Text

- Press `Backspace` or `Del` to delete a character.
- Select the text, and then press `Del`.
- Choose Select from the Edit menu, and then choose Sentence, Paragraph, All, Tabular Column, or Rectangle. Press `Del`.

Canceling a Deletion

1. Select Undelete from the Edit menu or press `Ctrl`+`Shift`+`Z`.
2. Select Restore, or select Next or Previous to view other recent deletions.

Using Undo

1. Select Undo from the Edit menu or press `Ctrl`+`Z`.

Selecting Text

- *With the keyboard:* position the insertion point, press `F8`, and complete the selection by moving the insertion point.
- *With the mouse:* press the left mouse button, hold it down, and drag it across the text to block.
- *With either keyboard or mouse:* choose Select from the Edit menu and identify the selection.

Chapter 3

Creating Your First Document

Now that WordPerfect for Windows is started and ready to go, you can start typing a document. This chapter covers how to create a new document, and how to enter codes to control the appearance of text in the document. Unless you never make a mistake, you'll find an opportunity to use the Typeover and Insert modes to edit your work. You'll also learn some editing basics such as deleting, blocking, moving, and copying, and a couple of important safeguards—Undelete and Undo—that can save you when you really mess up.

Just Start Typing!

When you start WordPerfect, an empty document file appears automatically for your use. The insertion point appears in the upper left of the screen. As you type, the characters appear on-screen at the insertion point.

Do not press ⏎Enter until you reach the end of a paragraph. Just continue typing, and the text will move automatically to the next line. This is called *word wrapping*. Then, when you edit the text later, the lines of text within the paragraph will readjust automatically to fit within the margins.

> **TIP:** If you want to keep words together on a line (such as a person's first and last name), you can enter a *hard space*. Delete any existing space between the words. Then, with your insertion point on the first letter of the second word, press Ctrl+Spacebar. Or, select Layout, Line, Other Codes, Hard Space. A space appears on your screen, and a Hard Space code is placed in the text. (Codes are covered in the next section.)

To practice entering text, type in the following example. [Enter] at the end of a line indicates that you should press ↵Enter. [Left Tab] indicates that you should press Tab⇥. When you are done, your screen should look like Figure 3.1.

Mr. David Randolph [Enter]
Vice President [Enter]
Bennington Corporation [Enter]
45 Superstition Highway [Enter]
Phoenix, Arizona 85251 [Enter]
[Enter]
Dear Mr. Randolph: [Enter]
[Enter]
[Left Tab] I am interested in pursuing a career with the Bennington Corporation.

Codes in Your Document

When you create a document—as you saw in entering the example text—you not only type letters and numbers, but you also press special keys (such as ↵Enter and Tab⇥) that affect the text.

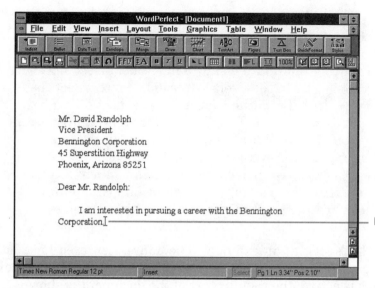

Figure 3.1
Sample text entered into the document screen.

Some word processing programs put codes on the screen to symbolize such actions, but having all those codes among the characters of your text can get confusing. WordPerfect hides its codes, without leaving odd symbols scattered around. You can see the codes through Reveal Codes. Handling the codes in this way provides two major benefits:

- There are no confusing symbols on your screen.

- Longer codes (instead of short-but-cryptic symbols) can be used, which fully explain the action taken.

Revealing and Hiding Codes

To see the codes, press Alt+F3 or select Reveal Codes from the View menu. The Reveal Codes area appears on the bottom of your screen. It not only shows the text in the document, but also each code entered. You can repeat the procedure to hide the codes again.

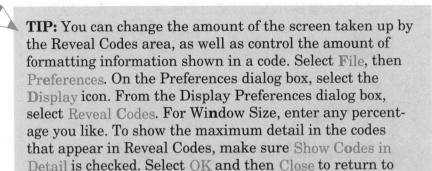

TIP: You can change the amount of the screen taken up by the Reveal Codes area, as well as control the amount of formatting information shown in a code. Select File, then Preferences. On the Preferences dialog box, select the Display icon. From the Display Preferences dialog box, select Reveal Codes. For Window Size, enter any percentage you like. To show the maximum detail in the codes that appear in Reveal Codes, make sure Show Codes in Detail is checked. Select OK and then Close to return to your document. You may also control the size of Reveal Codes by dragging the divider line with the mouse.

Let's look at an example. The address entered for a letter, along with Reveal Codes, is shown in Figure 3.2. When Reveal Codes is active, the regular text of the document is shown at the top of the screen. The same text, along with the codes, appears at the bottom of the screen. Notice these codes:

HRt

Left Tab

SRt

Figure 3.2
The address shown in the document screen and Reveal Codes.

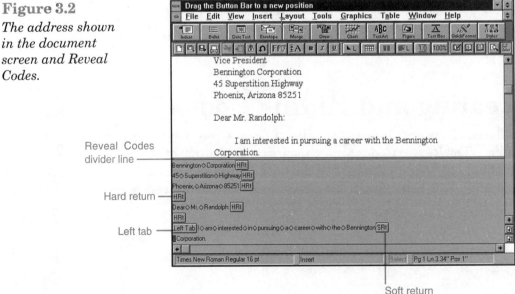

The **HRt** code stands for a *hard return*. This shows each place you have pressed ⏎Enter. The **Left Tab** code shows where Tab↹ was pressed. The **SRt** code stands for a *soft return*. This code is entered automatically by WordPerfect, and shows where each line wraps around.

It's a good idea to use Reveal Codes when you want to insert, cut, or copy text. This way, you can make sure the codes are handled properly along with the text. Reveal Codes is also helpful in tracking down formatting problems. If your text looks odd, you may have entered a code inadvertently. Just check Reveal Codes, and remove any unwanted codes. (Some codes expand to show more information when you place your insertion point before them.)

If you want to use the same codes over and over in a document, it may be faster to enter the keystrokes for the codes, and then copy the codes and paste them where you want them. For example, you may enter complex settings for a particular line or graphic that you want repeated. Instead of setting up the line or graphic from scratch each time you want it to appear in the document, copy the code and paste it in at later points in the document. (Copy, paste, line, and graphic functions are all covered later. For now, just keep this possibility in mind.)

Inserting and Deleting Codes

Although codes appear to be made up of individual characters, each is really a single entity. Therefore, you cannot edit codes the same way that you edit regular text. You can, however, insert and delete codes very easily.

- **To insert a code**, move the insertion point to the desired location, and then perform the action. The code for the action appears. For example, to insert a **HRt** code at the insertion point's location, just press ⏎Enter.

- **To delete a code**, move the insertion point before the code, and press `Del`.

    To close the Reveal Codes screen, press `Alt`+`F3` again, or select Reveal Codes from the View menu.

Insert and Typeover Modes

When you type text in *Insert mode*, existing text moves to the right to make room. (Insert mode is WordPerfect's default mode.) For example, in the sample letter shown in Figure 3.3, the phrase "As I mentioned in our conversation today" was inserted after the tab, and before the beginning of the existing sentence. The original sentence moved to the right and wrapped around automatically.

Figure 3.3

In Insert mode, old characters move over to make room for newly typed ones.

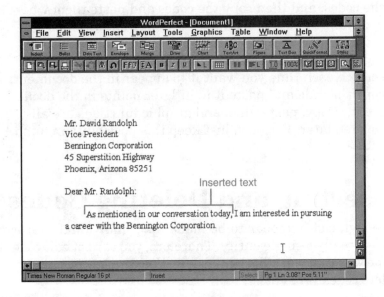

If you prefer, you can switch to *Typeover mode*, which means any characters you type will replace existing characters. Take a look at the letter in Figure 3.4. The word "discussed" was typed over the word "mentioned." To switch between Insert mode and Typeover mode, just press Ins. This key is called a *toggle key*, since pressing it will switch (that is, toggle) you between one option and another.

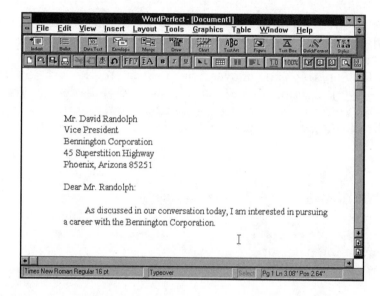

Figure 3.4

In Typeover mode, old characters are replaced by new ones.

TIP: Text that you type will never replace a code, even in Typeover mode. The code will simply move over, just as text does in Insert mode. The text is inserted before the code.

Deleting Text

One way to get rid of text—one character at a time—is to press ⬅Backspace; the character, space, or code to the left of the insertion point is deleted as the insertion point moves left. On many computers, you can hold down ⬅Backspace to continue deleting text until you release the key.

TIP: When you delete text, it is removed from the document. Because text in WordPerfect may contain codes as well as text and spaces, it is a good idea to turn on Reveal Codes when you delete. This way you can be assured that you're deleting precisely the text, spaces, or codes you want to delete.

Another way to delete text is to use the *Delete key*, marked `Del` on many keyboards. When you press `Del`, the character, space, or code after the insertion point is deleted, and all remaining text on the page moves one position to the left. As with `◆Backspace`, holding down `Del` on most keyboards repeats the delete. Your insertion point stays in position, and the text to the right of the insertion point moves to the left as you delete one character at a time.

TIP: To delete a word at the insertion point, press `Ctrl`+`◆Backspace` or `Ctrl`+`Del`. To delete from the insertion point to the end of a line, press `Ctrl`+`Del`. To delete to the end of the page, press `Ctrl`+`◆Shift`+`Del`.

Selecting Text

To delete, cut, or copy larger blocks of text, first you'll need to *select* the text. Selecting text marks the characters, spaces, and codes you want to manipulate. Selecting text is also used to perform other functions (such as centering a large amount of text). You can select text using the keyboard or mouse.

Using the mouse to select text is a popular method. Place the insertion point at one end of the text to be selected. Hold down the left mouse button, and drag the insertion point to the other end of the selected text. As you drag, the selected text appears *highlighted*. When you have the corrected text highlighted, release the left mouse button. The text is selected.

Suppose you aren't sure about David Randolph's actual title. Figure 3.5 shows the title "Vice President" selected. The insertion point was dragged from the V in "Vice President" to the B in "Bennington" on the following line. This was done to include the hard return code (**HRt**) at the end of the "Vice President" line.

Now take a look at Reveal Codes. Notice that **Select** appears at the beginning of the selection, and the insertion point is before the B in "Bennington." This indicates that the text after **Select** up to the "B" is selected.

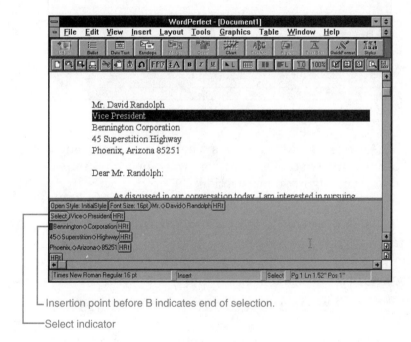

Figure 3.5
Text selected.

Once you have selected the text, you must immediately perform the delete, cut, or copy action. When you perform the delete, copy, or cut operation on the selected text, "Select" is grayed in the lower right corner of the screen. In the sample letter, for example, we are deleting the text—so we press ⏎Del. Figure 3.6 shows the result. Both the title and the hard return are deleted, and the lines below move up.

Figure 3.6
Selected text deleted.

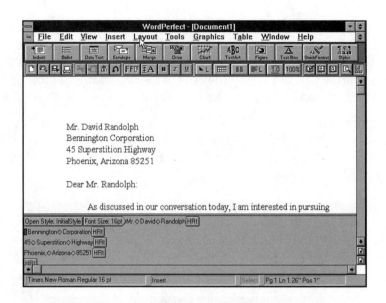

TIP: Always use Reveal Codes when you are selecting text that may involve codes. That way you won't miss important formatting in your selection.

The following Quick Steps summarize the process for selecting text with a mouse.

Selecting Text with the Mouse

1. Put the insertion point on the first character, space, or code you wish to select.	Your insertion point is positioned.
2. Hold down the left mouse button and drag the insertion point to the other end of the text.	The text is highlighted as it is selected.
3. Release the left mouse button.	The text is selected (appears highlighted).

If you want to use the keyboard to select text, position your insertion point and press F8. The **Select** code appears in Reveal Codes. Move the insertion point to complete the selection (use the movement key combinations described in Chapter 2). Table 3.1 lists other options for selecting blocks of text quickly.

Mouse

Point to	To select
A word and double-click	A word
A sentence and triple-click	A sentence
A paragraph and quadruple-click	A paragraph
A position and Í+click	From the position to the insertion point

Keyboard

Press	To select
⇧Shift+≥ or ≤	One character at a time
⇧Shift+↑ or ↓	A line at a time
⇧Shift+End	To the end of a line
⇧Shift+Home, Home	To the beginning of a line before codes
⇧Shift+PgUp or PgDn	To the top or then continue pressing bottom of the PgUp or PgDn screen, then screen by screen
⇧Shift+Alt+PgUp or PgDn	To the first line of the previous or next page
⇧Shift+Ctrl+← or →	One word at a time
⇧Shift+Ctrl+↑ or ↓	One paragraph at a time
⇧Shift+Ctrl+Home	To the beginning of a document after codes
⇧Shift+Ctrl+End	To the end of a document after codes

Table 3.1
Other Selection Techniques

If you make a selection and want to get out of it (that is, get rid of the highlight and continue with other work), press Esc or click outside the selected area. The selection disappears.

TIP: You may also use menus to make selections. Place the insertion point on text to include in the select. Choose Edit, then Select. You may select a **S**entence, **P**aragraph, **A**ll, Tabular **C**olumn, or **R**ectangle.

Many WordPerfect for Windows functions can be performed on selected text. Delete, copy, and cut were used as examples earlier in this chapter, but there are many more. These include (but are by no means limited to) character size and appearance, spell checking, printing, saving, searching, replacing, line spacing, and indenting.

Canceling Deletions (Undelete)

With WordPerfect, you can afford an "oops" when you delete, as long as you restore the text before making three other deletions. WordPerfect stores the most recent three deletions.

To restore a deletion, follow these steps:

1. Place your insertion point where you want the text to be restored.

2. Press Ctrl+⇧Shift+Z, or select Undelete from the Edit menu. When you undelete, you can select among the last three deletions and restore your selection. On the Undelete dialog box, these options appear: **R**estore, **N**ext, and **P**revious.

3. Continue to select Next or Previous until the deletion you want to restore appears. Then, select Restore to insert that deleted text.

There's a limit to the amount of deleted material WordPerfect can remember. If you make an unusually large deletion, WordPerfect will ask you:

Delete without saving for Undelete?(Y/N)

This message means you can go ahead and make your deletion, but it won't be available to be undeleted through Ctrl+⇧Shift+Z or Undelete from the Edit menu.

Using Undo

Undo can be used to reverse your last editing activity, such as entering or deleting text, adding graphics, or changing formatting. Text is restored to its original location. To undo, press Ctrl+Z, or select Undo from the Edit menu.

TIP: Don't confuse Undo with Undelete. They are very different. Undo reverses your last editing action and restores text to its original position. When you use Undelete, on the other hand, any of the last three deletions can be restored at the current location of the insertion point.

Not all activities can be undone with Undo. Complex activities like sorting, generating lists, and the like cannot be undone. To protect your original work before performing a complex editing activity, save your file before performing the work. Then, if you don't like the result, you can undo the work by exiting your file without saving it, and then using the original (saved) file. Learn more about saving documents in the next chapter.

CAUTION

Cutting and Pasting Text (Moving)

You can move a sentence, paragraph, page, or block of text at a time. When you move text, it is *cut* (removed) from the location from which you are moving, and placed in the *Clipboard* (a temporary storage area within Windows). It is then available to *paste* into the original document, a new document, or another Windows application. In fact, the text you cut to the Clipboard stays there until you cut or copy other text to the Clipboard, or leave WordPerfect for Windows.

Figure 3.7 and 3.8 show how text looks before and after a cut-and-paste job. Notice that the last sentence and the second sentence have been transposed. This operation required the following: First, the sentence My complete résumé is attached. was selected, along with the space before the sentence. Then Edit, Cut was selected. This placed the text in the Clipboard. The insertion point was moved to after the period of the sentence ending "...Bennington Corporation." With the insertion point marking the spot where the space and sentence would be placed, Edit, Paste was selected. The text was moved from the Clipboard to the paragraph, and inserted at the location of the insertion point.

Figure 3.7

Text before cutting and pasting.

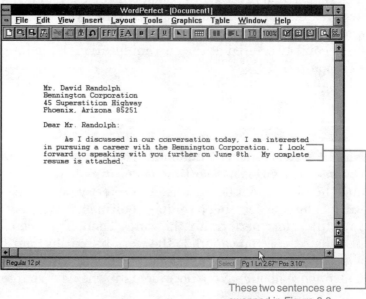

These two sentences are swapped in Figure 3.8.

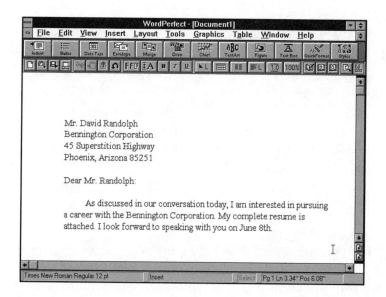

Figure 3.8
*Text after cutting
and pasting.*

In general, to cut text, you can use any one of these three methods:

- Select Edit, Cut.
- Press Ctrl+X.
- Select the Cut button on the Power Bar.

To paste text, use one of these three methods:

- Select Edit, Paste.
- Press Ctrl+V.
- Select the Paste button on the Power Bar.

To perform a cut-and-paste operation, use the following Quick Steps:

Cutting and Pasting Text

1. Select the text to be cut.   The text is highlighted.

2. Select Edit, Cut, or press Ctrl+X, or select the Cut button on the Power Bar.   The text selected for the cut operation is placed in the Clipboard.

continues

---

continued

3. Place the insertion point at the location where you want to paste the text.

The insertion point marks where text on the Clipboard will go.

4. Select Edit, Paste or press ⌐Shift⌐+ V or select the Paste button from the Power Bar.

The text from the Clipboard appears in the document at the insertion point.

TIP: You can use the Quick Menu to paste and perform other operations. The *Quick Menu* is a fast way to get at often-used operations. Just press the right mouse button. The Quick Menu appears. Make any selections you desire.

Copying and Pasting Text

Copying is similar to cutting text, except that the selected text remains in the document, and a copy goes to the Clipboard for later pasting.

Figure 3.9 illustrates a copy operation. Notice that the address line "45 Superstition Highway" was copied into a sentence that was added to the body of the letter, as follows: The following sentence was entered:

I'll meet you at your corporate office location at .

A space and a period were included at the end of the sentence. Once this text was entered, the address was copied. To begin the copy, the address (minus city, state, and Zip code) was selected. Reveal Codes was used to make sure that the hard return at the end of the address was not included in the selection. Once the address was selected, Edit, Copy was chosen. The text remained in the letter and a copy was placed on the Clipboard. The insertion point was then moved between the space and period in the new sentence, to mark the location for the paste. Edit, Paste was selected, and the address was successfully copied.

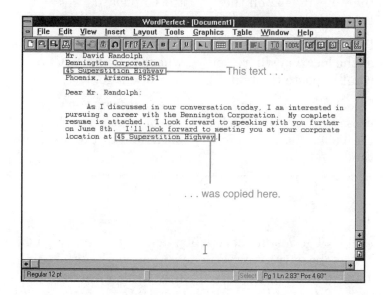

Figure 3.9
Copying text.

In general, to copy text, you can use any one of these three methods:

- Select Edit, Copy.
- Press Ctrl + C
- Select the Copy button on the Power Bar.

After you have copied text, paste the copy into its new location at the insertion point. To copy and paste text, use the following Quick Steps.

Copying a Block of Text

1. Select the text to be copied.   The text is highlighted.

continues

continued

2. Select Edit, Copy or press Ctrl+C, or select the Copy button on the Power Bar.

The text selected for the copy operation is placed in the Clipboard.

3. Place the insertion point at the location where you want to paste the text.

The insertion point marks where text on the Clipboard will go.

4. Select Edit, Paste or press Ctrl+V or select the Paste button from the Power Bar.

The text from the Clipboard appears in the document at the insertion point.

CAUTION The results of copying, deleting, or moving can be surprising. Whenever you work with copying or moving text and you are unsure of the outcome, save your work first with Ctrl+S. Then, if the outcome isn't as you expected, your original document is available. Chapter 4, "Saving, Opening, and Exiting Documents," covers the ways to save a document.

FYI IDEAS There are several hidden uses for copying. Copy to reduce mistakes, to repeat a line of text for a particular effect, or to streamline formats represented by codes.

Copying is handy when you want to make sure you don't introduce mistakes when existing information is repeated in a document. For example, it is easy to enter incorrectly such data as an address, account number, or unusual proper name. Assuming the first occurrence of the text is correct, copy that occurrence to ensure the other occurrences are correct, as well. Just enter the first occurrence of the text, then copy it as needed.

Copying can also be useful to repeat a particular line of text. For example, if you are making a sign-in sheet for a meeting, create a line with tabs and underlines for the necessary information (such as name, phone number, and so on). Then copy that line to add a second line. Next, copy two lines to make four lines, and so on until you create a complete page of underlines for the sign-in sheet. This approach saves you the tedium of setting up the tabs and underlines in each line, and ensures all lines are the same length.

Finally, save time and use copying to repeat formatting (or other settings held in codes). For example, you might have created a particular tab setting, then changed to a new tab setting later in the document. If you want to go back to the original tab setting later, just copy the **[Tab Set:]** code to the desired spot.

Using Drag-And-Drop to Move and Copy

After you see how easy this is, you'll wish you had skipped the last several pages and jumped straight to this procedure. If you're a mouse user, you can avoid all the menus and buttons by using drag-and-drop to move and copy.

1. Select the text that you want to move or copy with your mouse.

2. Position the mouse cursor on the selection, and click and hold down the left mouse button.

3. (Optional) If you want to copy, hold down the Ctrl key on the keyboard. (Skip this if you want to move.)

4. Drag the selection to its new location.

Appending to the Clipboard

Sometimes you may want to add text to the end of the Clipboard without losing the Clipboard's contents. For example, you may want to write a summary of a report. The information for the summary is scattered through the report. Consolidating the information for the summary is easy: Simply review the report start to finish, and as you go, Append the selected text to the Clipboard. When you are done, just Paste the Clipboard contents to a new location, and edit as necessary. Finding all the occurrences of the text you want, and placing them in the Clipboard in one pass, is much faster than copying each occurrence individually to the new location.

To Append to the Clipboard, select the text or graphics to append, and then choose Edit, Append. The text remains in your document, and is added to the end of the Clipboard. It remains there until you cut or copy other text to the Clipboard, or until you leave WordPerfect for Windows.

Switching Between View Modes

WordPerfect for Windows has several modes in which you can view documents. They are:

- **Draft:** WYSIWYG (What You See Is What You Get); text appears as it will when printed, including italics, bold, and special fonts. This view is faster to use than Page.

- **Page:** Includes the WYSIWYG characteristics of Draft view, and adds headers, footers, and certain formatting features.

- **Two Page:** Just like Page view, except two pages are shown.

To use a view, select View, then select a view and check it to make sure it is the one desired. To change the view, just select a new one.

In Draft and Page view, you can *zoom* in and out—that is, change the size of the display to show more (or less) detail. To zoom, select View, Zoom. On the Zoom dialog box, identify the percent of the magnification (or the amount of width) to display.

Creating Another New Document

WordPerfect allows you to have more than one document available at a time. Documents are stored in *document windows*. (Consult Chapter 13, "Managing Documents," for details on how to handle up to nine possible windows.) For now, just be aware that you can use the New command on the File menu to create a new document, without having to exit other documents. To create a new document, select New from the File menu. WordPerfect takes you to a new, blank document window. You can move between the two documents by selecting Window, then the document to which you want to go. For more information about handling multiple documents, see Chapter 13.

Ways to Save Your Work

- Press F3, or select Save As from the File menu.
- Press Ctrl+S or select Save from the File menu.
- Press Ctrl+F4 or select Close from the File menu.
- Press Alt+F4 or select Exit from the File menu.

Rules for Saving

- Name a document to save, using up to eight characters (optionally followed by a period and a three-character extension).
- Get in the habit of saving your work often.

Opening a Document

- Press Ctrl+O, or select Open from the File menu, and enter or select the path and filename.

Inserting a File

1. Position your insertion point where the document should appear.
2. Select Insert, File then enter or select the path and filename.

Viewing a Document

1. Use any of the following commands: File Open, File Save As, or Insert File.
2. Enter or select the first document to view, then select View.

Chapter 4

Saving, Opening, and Closing Documents

Once you have learned how to create a document, you will want to protect your document. The best way is to know how to save and close it properly. (Hint: turning the computer's power off is *not* the proper method of closing a document!)

Why You Must Save Your Work

Save your work or you lose it. As you work on a document, it is stored in a temporary storage space called *RAM*, which is only available as long as there is power to the computer. When the power is cut off (even accidentally for a split second), the data in RAM is lost. When you save a document, you copy it from RAM to a disk, where the data remains safe even when the power is off.

TIP: Because accidents happen to disks, too, saving a document to more than one disk is your insurance that the document will be available, even if one disk is lost or damaged.

Nearly every computer user can tell you a story of working for hours or days on an important document, but forgetting to save it—then losing the entire document when the power flickered or the wrong keys were accidentally pressed. Always take time to save your work. Develop these good habits:

- Periodically save your work as you go. That way, if the power to your computer fails, you will have a recent, complete version of your work. Any time you have entered edits that are significant (and that you wouldn't want to lose), save your work.

- Always save more than one copy of your document on more than one disk. Disks can be damaged or lost.

- Use WordPerfect for Windows' automatic backup options. WordPerfect has options that make copies of your most recent edits automatically as you work. They are explained later in this chapter.

Choosing a Name for Your Document

Before you save a document, you must choose a unique name for it. Follow these guidelines.

Names can be up to eight characters long. If you enter a name longer than eight characters, WordPerfect automatically cuts off the characters beyond eight.

WordPerfect for Windows automatically assigns the eight-character name an extension of *wpd*. For example, a document might be named **MYDOC123**, and WordPerfect for Windows will add **.WPD**. The document's full name is **MYDOC123.WPD**.

When naming a document, you can use:

- Letters A through Z

- Numbers 0 through 9

- Special characters such as ! @ # $$$ % ^ & ( ) - _ { }

Some special characters *cannot* be used in filenames, because they have other specific purposes. They are:

* + = [ ] : ; ~ ? / \ , (space)

If you attempt to use a symbol that WordPerfect for Windows won't accept, you'll receive a message like this (*filename* shows where the offending name appears):

This filename is invalid: *filename*

Do not use a period in a filename, because it will be mistaken for the divider between the name and the extension.

Each document must have a unique name. You can save the same document under many different names if you want multiple copies. Its a good idea to give a document a name that suggests the use of the document. Here are some examples:

LETDAVE1.WPD: The first letter to Dave.

LETDAVE2.WPD: The second letter to Dave.

IBBRPTV1.WPD: IBB Report, Version 1.

ME060893.WPD: Memo of 6/8/93.

Saving Your Work

Save your work as you go. Save every time you have performed edits you would hate to lose. Most users save their work every 15 minutes or so. Here's how to do it.

From the document, select Save from the File menu or press Ctrl + S. A dialog box like the one shown in Figure 4.1 appears.

Figure 4.1

Dialog box to save a document.

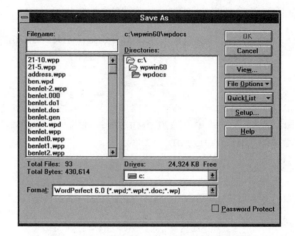

Type in the drive letter, path, and new document name, and press ⏎Enter. (The drive, path, and document name will appear automatically if the document has already been saved.) Select OK and the document is saved.

In this example, to save the letter to the Bennington Corporation, we use drive **C:\WPWIN60\WPDOCS** as the directory (the default document subdirectory set up when WordPerfect for Windows is installed), and **BENLET.WPD** as the document name.

If you want to enter a password to protect the document, you may check the Password Protect check box on the Save As dialog box. If you checked the **P**assword Protect check box, you will be asked to enter a password twice before the save operation is complete. Once a password is assigned, you'll have to enter the password every time you access the document. If you forget the password, you will not be able to access the document.

> **NOTE:** If you do not specify a drive and directory when you enter the document's filename, your document will be saved to the default document directory: usually C:\WPWIN60\WPDOCS. Saving your files to WPDOCS allows you to locate your files easily later. As you accumulate more document files, you may want to organize them into multiple directories, with separate directories for different projects or clients. Chapter 13, "Managing Documents," covers how to create directories of your own.

If you had already saved the document by selecting **F**ile, **S**ave (or pressing Ctrl+S), the file would have been quickly saved without going through the Save As dialog box.

The following Quick Steps summarize the process of saving a document.

Saving a Document

1. Select Save from the File menu, or press Ctrl+S.

   If this is the first time you've saved the document, a dialog box appears for the document name. (Otherwise the document is saved immediately.)

2. Type the drive letter, path, and document name, as necessary, and select OK.

   The document is saved.

Using Save As

After you've saved a document once, WordPerfect remembers its name and location, and saves the new version on top of the old one each time you save. If you want to save the new version under a different name (or in a different location), use Save As instead.

To use Save As, press F3, or select Save As from the File menu. A dialog box identical to the one in Figure 4.1 appears. You can enter a new drive, path, and filename, and then select OK, or just select OK if you decide to keep the old name.

Creative Uses of Save As

If you need multiple versions of the same document, use F3 or Save As from the File menu to create them. Simply give each version a related name. If you are working on a budget report, for example, and want to save three different versions—each with a different organization—you could name them BRPTVER1.WPD, BRPTVER2.WPD, and BRPTVER3.WPD.

You can also use Save As to create a backup of a file. To do this, save the same document to multiple locations. For example, you may want to save to a floppy disk, as well as to your hard disk. First, save to your hard disk with Save As from the File menu. Then, use F3 or Save As from the File menu again, this time entering the path for the floppy disk drive. In effect, you have just created a floppy disk backup of the file on the hard disk.

Saving Documents in Other Formats

If you exchange work with other users of personal computers, or send documents over the phone lines via a modem, you may need to put your document file in another format. You may also need to convert a different format into one WordPerfect for Windows can use.

To convert a WordPerfect file to another format, just use the Save **As** command with an additional step. After pressing F3 or selecting Save As from the File menu, type in a name for the document that suggests its format. For example, while the last three characters of BENLET.WPD suggests a WordPerfect for Windows document (if you used that convention), BENLET.TXT would suggest the file is saved in ASCII Text format for modem transmission. Once the name is typed in, select the Format option, and choose from one of the more than 50 formats available. After selecting a format, continue with the Save As procedure as usual.

Saving and Closing the Document

Instead of saving the document and continuing, you can close the document and save it as you go. Follow these Quick Steps.

Saving and Closing a Document

1. Press Ctrl+F4, or select Close from the File menu.

   A dialog box appears, asking whether you want to save the changes to the document.

2. Respond Yes to save the changes, or No to lose the changes since the most recent save.

   The document is closed.

CAUTION — *Never turn off the computer while in WordPerfect for Windows.* This can damage your document or WordPerfect software. Always use Alt+F4 or File, Exit to leave. If you have forgotten to save your document, WordPerfect will prompt you before exiting.

Saving Part of a Document

You can save just a part of a document, if you want. This is useful when you want to delete the rest of the document. It is also useful when you want to place part of a document in a new document with a unique name. (This procedure creates a new document, made up of a portion of the existing document.) Follow these Quick Steps:

QUICK STEPS

Saving Part of a Document

1. Use F8 or the mouse to select the part of the document you want to save.

   The part to be saved becomes highlighted.

2. Press F3, or select Save As from the File menu.

   The Save dialog box appears.

3. Identify that you want to save the Selected Text (versus the Entire File) and select OK.

   The Save As dialog box appears.

4. Type in the name of the document, and press ↵Enter or select OK. (Include the drive and path designation, if necessary.)

   The text block from the existing document is saved under the new name, and you are returned to your original document.

Using Automatic Backup

If you save your documents regularly, they will be protected from power loss or system failure. To provide additional protection for the forgetful, WordPerfect for Windows has an automatic *backup* option. (You will still want to use **S**ave often, in order to save your entire document.) There are two automatic backup functions:

- **Timed Document Backup:** The document on your screen is saved every ten minutes (or at intervals you specify) in a temporary file. When you exit WordPerfect properly, all temporary files are deleted, but if the power is accidentally cut off, the temporary files remain, and you can often retrieve a portion of your work from them.

- **Original Document Backup:** When you save a document or exit WordPerfect, the last disk version of the document is saved in a file with a .BK! extension, rather than being replaced by the new version.

To set up automatic backup options, follow these Quick Steps.

Backup Options Setup

1. Select File, Preferences.

   The Preferences dialog box appears.

2. Select the File icon.

   The File Preferences dialog box (shown in Figure 4.2) appears.

3. To use the Timed Backup feature, check the Timed Document Backup every xx minutes. (In the text box, fill in the number of minutes between each backup.)

   The Timed Backup options are set.

continues

continued

4. Check Original Document Backup to create backup files of each document. (You can deselect the option to omit keeping backup files for each document.)	The option is set.
5. Select OK, then Close.	You are returned to your document.

Figure 4.2

The File Preferences dialog box.

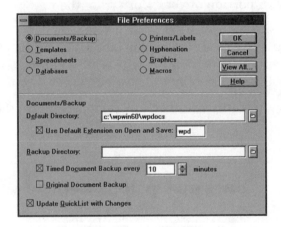

Recovering an Automatically Saved Document

If you use timed backup and you experience a computer power failure, you may be able to recover the timed-backup copy of your document. Just restart WordPerfect for Windows. The Timed Backup dialog box appears, with a message like:

- **Choose one of the following activities:**

- Rename the document to create a file.

- **O**pen to open the document (then, potentially, save the document).

- **D**elete to lose the contents of the backup file.

> Don't give the recovered backup file the same name as the original file in which you were working, in case the original file is a more complete copy.   **CAUTION**

Open and Insert: What's the Difference?

Opening and inserting a file both refer to moving the document from disk storage into RAM (and onto the screen). *Opening* a document inserts it into a new document window. *Inserting a file* places the contents of the file in the current document window, which may or may not include existing text. You can also *view* a document without either opening or inserting it.

Opening a Document

To open a document, follow these steps.

QUICK STEPS

Opening a Document

1. Press [Ctrl]+[O], or select **O**pen from the **F**ile menu.   The Open File dialog box appears.

2. In the Open File dialog box, enter or select the path and filename of the document you want to open. Select OK.   The document is opened in a new window.

An alternative to typing in the path and filename is to select the drive, directory, and filename. You may use the mouse or the [Tab⇄] key to move to each area of the Open File dialog box. Select between Drives as necessary. Then, select the correct directory in the Directories list. When you click on (or select) a directory, the file icon appears open. The Filename list shows the files for the directory you selected. Choose a file by name.

CAUTION   The Filename text box contains the default filename *.* (this means that files will be shown automatically). To show all files that end with **wpd** in the selected directory, enter *.**wpd** in the Filename text box, and press [⏎Enter]. Using this technique, you may also display only the files that start with a certain character (or characters), or files with other extensions. For example, entering LET*.* will display all files that start with LET, regardless of the rest of the filename. Entering *.TXT will display all files that end with the TXT file extension.

Using QuickFinder to Find the Document

If you're not sure where you saved a file, or what it was called, you're up a creek. Or rather, you *would* be if WordPerfect did not provide QuickFinder. Follow these steps to find the file you seek. (You'll learn more about QuickFinder later in the book.)

1. Choose **Q**uickFinder from the **F**ile menu. The QuickFinder dialog box appears.

2. If you remember part or all of the file's name, enter it in the File **P**attern text box. You can use wild cards for the part you don't recall. For example, if you are sure the file began with M, enter M*.*. If you are sure the file had 6 letters, enter ??????.*.

3. If you don't know the name of the file but remember that it contained certain text, type that text in the **S**earch For text box.

4. Click the Search **I**n button and select where you want the search to occur. Disk is a good choice if you know the file is somewhere on your hard disk.

5. Click the **F**ind button.

6. If such a file (or more than one) is found, a Search Results list dialog box will open. Under Search Results, highlight the file you're looking for, and select the Open button. The file opens.

Inserting a File

You can insert a file into a blank document window or into an existing document. Follow these Quick Steps.

Inserting a File

1. Place your insertion point where you want the document to be inserted. Select Insert.

   The Insert pull-down menu appears.

2. Select File.

   The Insert File dialog box appears.

3. Type in or select the path and document name, and select Insert.

   The document is inserted at the insertion point.

CAUTION When you type in a filename you want to open or insert, and then proceed, you may see a dialog box with a message like this:

This file does not exist:
C:\WPWIN60\WPDOCS*filename*

This means that one of the following has occurred:

- You have made a typographical error in the document drive, directory, or name.

- The information is incorrect.

- The file does not exist on the disk.

Whatever the reason, WordPerfect for Windows cannot match the information you provided with a document on the disk. If, after carefully checking your typing accuracy, you cannot determine the problem, it may be that you've forgotten the document name. Check the drive, directory, and files selected according to the entry in the Filename text box. Visually locate the file you need. (You can use the View feature described in this chapter to scan existing file contents quickly, and locate the file you want.)

Saving Typing with Inserting a File

If you have a document on the screen, and then insert another, the one you are inserting is placed in the current document at the position of your insertion point. This feature is useful for loading boilerplate text into a document. *Boilerplate* is any text that you use over and over, such as an address or greeting.

Let's say you've typed a letter and want to retrieve the boilerplate text **Sincerely, Barbara J. Wiley**, from a document called CLOSE.WPD. Just position the insertion point at the end of the letter, and use **I**nsert **F**ile.

Viewing a Document

You may view documents without opening or inserting them into windows. You cannot edit a document you are viewing, although you can view documents in order. This feature is handy if you want a quick look at one or more documents without having to wait for each to be opened (and, later, closed).

To view a document, use any of the following commands: File Open, File Save As, or Insert File. On the dialog box which appears, enter or select the name of the file you want to view, then choose the View command button. The Viewer (shown in Figure 4.3) appears.

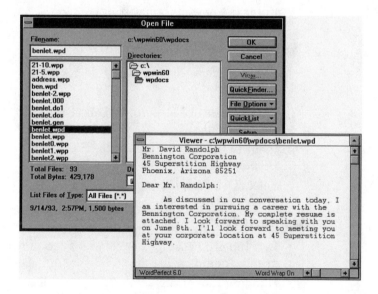

Figure 4.3
The Viewer.

Use the scroll bar or the ↓ and ↑ to move through the document. To view another document, select it on the Filename list. Or, with the Filename list selected, press the ↑ or the ↓ to view the next (or previous) document. To close the Viewer, open the Control Menu and select Close, or press Alt+F4.

Selecting Paper Size

1. Select Page, then Paper Size, from the Layout menu.
2. Select the paper size.

Changing the Margins

1. Press Ctrl+F8, or select Margins from the Layout menu.
2. Enter the new margin settings.

Changing the Unit of Measure

1. Select Preferences from the File menu.
2. Select Display.
3. Select Units of Measure, and enter the type of measurement.
4. Identify the unit for the Status Bar/Ruler Display.
5. Select OK, then Close.

Aligning Text

- Left Indent: Press F7, or select Layout, Paragraph, Indent.
- Hanging Indent: Press Ctrl+F7, or select Layout, Paragraph, Hanging Indent.
- Double (Right and Left) Indent: Press Ctrl+⇧Shift+F7, or select Layout, Paragraph, Double Indent.
- Back Tab: Select Layout, Paragraph, Back Tab.
- Center Text: Press ⇧Shift+F7, or select Layout, Line, Center.
- Flush Right: Press Alt+F7, or select Layout, Line, Flush Right.

Justifying Text

1. Select Layout, then Justification.
2. Select the type of justification.

Margins and Alignment

Where the text appears on the page is easy to control with WordPerfect. You can set the size of margins, control the size and type of paper, use a variety of units of measure, and print "sideways" on a page. You can also control the alignment of the text in relation to those margins. This chapter will teach you how to do all these things and more.

What's a Margin?

Margins are the amount of space from the edge of the paper to the text in your document. WordPerfect allows you to determine the size of your margins document by document. You can change margins within a document as often as you like.

NOTE: Most WordPerfect users like to use inches to measure the margins. You may enter other units of measure, however, as described at the end of this chapter.

Controlling margins is a two-step procedure:

- **Enter the paper size and type.** This tells WordPerfect the dimensions of your paper. (A printer must be selected before you can do this. Typically, you select a printer when WordPerfect is set up. If not, see Chapter 7, "Printing Your Work.")

- **Identify the size of each margin:** top, bottom, left, and right. WordPerfect will leave the margins as "white space."

WordPerfect fits your text into the space that remains. As a result, the line length of the text you enter is determined by the measurement from the left to the right of the page, minus the left and right margins. The number of lines that WordPerfect fits on a page is determined by the length of the page minus the top and bottom margins.

Figure 5.1 shows the edge of the paper, the margins, and the area for WordPerfect to use for a letter.

Figure 5.1

Margins are the areas between the paper edge and the document area.

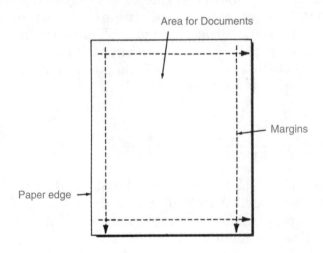

Area for Documents

Margins

Paper edge

Setting the Paper Size and Type

The first step in controlling margins is to set the paper size and type. The *default* (the setting that comes already established in WordPerfect) is 8.5-by-11-inch paper of standard weight. This default handles most common stationery, computer or typing paper. For most work, you won't need to change the default settings. In fact, if you happen to use paper of a size other than 8.5 by 11 inches, or a different type (such as envelopes, letterhead, transparencies, labels, or cardstock), you will need to change only the paper size or type.

> **TIP:** More than one *Paper Size / Type code* can appear in a document. The code affects all the text that follows. You could, for example, have a letter on a page, and then switch the Paper Size/Type to include the envelope on the next page. Just make sure the correct paper or envelope is available when printing.

To specify a different paper size or type for the document you are creating, follow these Quick Steps.

Changing the Paper Size or Type

1. Place the cursor at the top of the page for which the new paper size will take effect.

2. Select Page from the   A cascading menu appears.
   Layout menu.

continues

continued

3. Select Paper Size.

The Paper Size dialog box (shown in Figure 5.2) appears.

4. In the Paper Size dialog box, highlight the Paper Name.

The Information and Orientation visual appears at the bottom of the dialog box, describing the paper.

5. Choose Select.

You are returned to your document.

Figure 5.2

The Paper Size / Type dialog box.

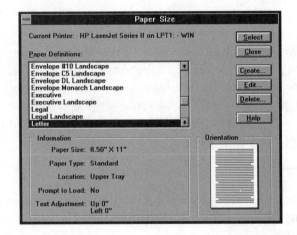

A code like the following one is placed in your document, and may be viewed using Reveal Codes with the insertion point on the code: Paper Sz/Typ: 8.5" by 11", Letter.

Understanding Landscape Printing

All printers print in *portrait orientation* (such as a typical business letter, where text is parallel to the short edge of the paper, and envelopes are fed with the wide edge first). Yours may also allow for *landscape orientation* (or sideways, with print parallel to the long edge of the paper). This is useful for printing text in wide columns, or envelopes fed with the narrow edge first. Figure 5.3 illustrates these two print orientations: a typical letter, and an envelope that accompanies the letter.

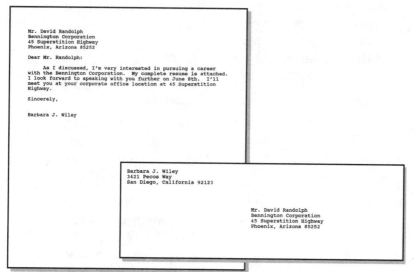

Figure 5.3

Portrait printing for a letter, and landscape printing for its envelope.

TIP: Landscape printing is useful for a document such as a list or chart with a left margin that is too long to fit on a sheet of paper 8.5 inches wide. If you print the document in landscape orientation, more text is allowed on a line.

Setting Margins

In WordPerfect, the right, left, top, and bottom margins are all set to one inch unless you change them. The following Quick Steps detail the procedure.

Setting Document Margins

1. Place the insertion point where you want the margin settings to take effect. To affect the entire document, place the insertion point at the beginning.

   The code will be inserted at this spot.

2. Press Ctrl + F8 or select Margins on the Layout menu.

   The Margin dialog box appears.

3. Enter all settings for Left, Right, Top, and Bottom.

   The visual page layout sample changes as you change the settings.

4. When all settings are final, select OK.

   A code is inserted in your document like this: **Lft Mar:2"**, and the margins take effect. Text occurring after this code will be affected.

Figure 5.4 shows our letter with one-inch margins, WordPerfect's default. Figure 5.5 shows the letter after the margins have been changed to 2 inches. The lines in the letter are shortened and wrap around to accommodate the new, wider margins.

Here's a quick guide to printing on letterhead paper. Measure how far down from the top of the letterhead the text must fall. Set your top margin at this measure. Measure how far from the bottom of the letterhead text should stop for a pleasing effect. This distance is the number to enter for your bottom margin.

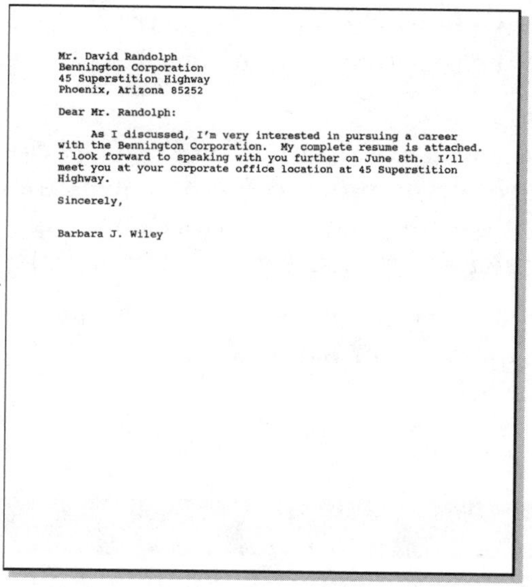

Mr. David Randolph
Bennington Corporation
45 Superstition Highway
Phoenix, Arizona 85252

Dear Mr. Randolph:

As I discussed, I'm very interested in pursuing a career with the Bennington Corporation. My complete resume is attached. I look forward to speaking with you further on June 8th. I'll meet you at your corporate office location at 45 Superstition Highway.

Sincerely,

Barbara J. Wiley

Figure 5.4
A letter with one-inch margins.

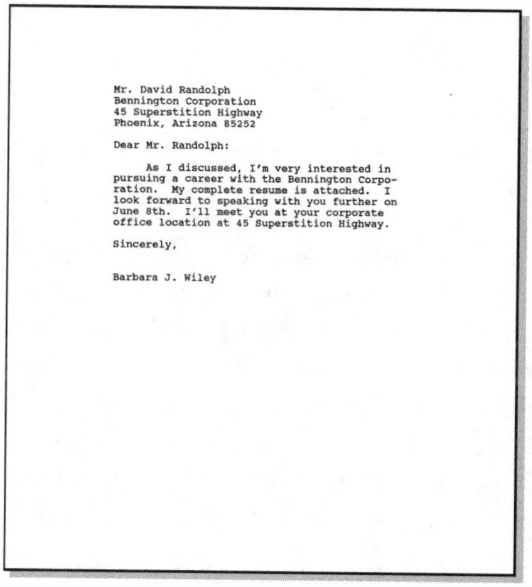

Mr. David Randolph
Bennington Corporation
45 Superstition Highway
Phoenix, Arizona 85252

Dear Mr. Randolph:

As I discussed, I'm very interested in pursuing a career with the Bennington Corpo-ration. My complete resume is attached. I look forward to speaking with you further on June 8th. I'll meet you at your corporate office location at 45 Superstition Highway.

Sincerely,

Barbara J. Wiley

Figure 5.5
A letter with two-inch margins.

Setting the Unit of Measure

The *status line* identifies the location of your cursor in inches. For example, these status-line values

Ln 2" Pos 5"

indicate that the line on which your cursor rests is two inches from the top edge of the paper, and five inches from the left edge of the paper.

Most people who use WordPerfect keep *inches* as the default unit of measure for margins and other measurements. Using inches makes it easy to place characters on a page, because you can pick up a ruler and measure margins or other format options.

You may, however, have a special need for another unit of measure. The units of measure available in WordPerfect are shown in Table 5.1.

Table 5.1
WordPerfect's Measurement Unit Options

Measurement	Notation
Inches	"
Centimeters	c
Millimeters	m
Points	p
1200ths of an inch	w

When you specify a particular type of measurement (such as a margin entry), you can enter the amount of the measurement, followed by its notation. If you set the default as inches, the entry is converted to inches. For example, if you want a right margin to be four centimeters, enter **4c** in the Right Margin field. If the default is inches, WordPerfect converts four centimeters to 1.57 inches, and displays that amount. If you are using a laser printer, you may want to use *points* occasionally. These units are used to measure the size of type; one point equals 1/72-inch.

WordPerfect allows you to control the unit of measure used in menus or displayed in the status line. Simply change the default.

To change the default for the unit of measurement, follow these steps:

1. Select Preferences from the File menu.

2. Select Display.

3. From the Display Preferences dialog box, select the Units of Measure drop-down list, and select the unit of measurement desired. The unit is set.

4. On the Display Preferences dialog box, select the Status Bar/Ruler Display drop-down list, and enter the unit of measurement. The unit is set for display on the status bar and ruler (the latter is most useful for setting tabs, and is covered in Chapter 8).

5. Select OK, then Close to return to your document. The new defaults are set.

Overview of Aligning Text

Though you can align text the old-fashioned way (using the (Spacebar) to place characters), there are faster methods that yield more pleasing results (which are easier to alter). A few key presses allow you to indent, center, justify, and place text flush right. You can also control line spacing, and set initial codes to specify your own default settings; these features can save you time when you create new documents.

Indenting Text

Using WordPerfect's *indent* feature is different from using the (Tab⇄) key. When you use (Tab⇄), only the first line is indented. When you use WordPerfect's indent feature, you indent the entire paragraph. You can type as many lines as you want, and then press (⤶Enter) to end the paragraph (and the indention).

There are four types of indents you can use in WordPerfect:

- **Indent** (*left indent*): The entire paragraph is indented a certain distance from the left margin.

- **Hanging indent:** The first line of the paragraph aligns with the left margin, but subsequent lines are indented.

- **Double Indent** (*left and right indent*)**:** The entire paragraph is indented a certain distance from both the left and right margins.

- **Back Tab:** The text does a reverse indent, aligning to the left of the current setting, even farther left than the left margin.

These four types of indents are shown in Figure 5.6.

All indents align with the tab settings in WordPerfect. For now, you should work with the default tab settings. (Chapter 8 "Tabs, Columns, and Tables," covers how to change tab settings.)

The following Quick Steps summarize each kind of indent.

QUICK STEPS

Setting the Left Indent

1. Press F7 (or select Paragraph, then Indent from the Layout menu) until the you reach the appropriate tab setting.

   An *Indent code* is embedded in your text. The **Hd Lft Ind** code appears.

2. Type in the text you want indented.

   The text aligns automatically with the last indent entered. Any text in the paragraph immediately following the indent is indented.

3. Press ↵Enter to complete the indent.

QUICK STEPS

Setting a Hanging Indent

1. Press Ctrl+F7 or select Paragraph and then Hanging Indent from the Layout menu.

   The codes **Hd Lft Ind** and **Hd Back Tab** are placed in your text.

2. Type in the text.

The first line remains at the left margin, and subsequent lines are indented.

3. Press ⏎Enter.

TIP: To create a bulleted list, select the Bullet button on the Button Bar. The Bullets & Numbers dialog box appears. Select the symbol of the bullet, then OK. Type in the text, and press ⏎Enter when you are done with the bulleted item.

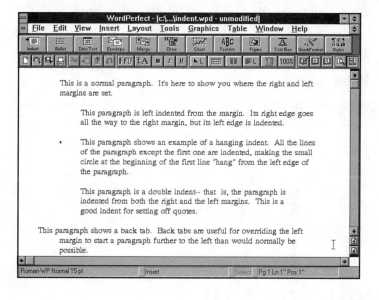

Figure 5.6
Text with indents.

Setting a Double Indent

1. Press Ctrl + ⇧Shift + F7 (or select Paragraph, then Double Indent from the Layout menu).

The code **Hd Left/Right Ind** is placed in your text.

continues

continued

2. Type in the text.	The text aligns along the left tab setting, at an equal distance from the right side.
3. Press `Enter` to complete the indent.	The text that follows the double indent is set in from the left and right margins.

QUICK STEPS

Setting a Back Tab

1. Select Paragraph, then Back Tab from the Layout menu.	The code **Hd Back Tab** is placed in your text.

2. Type in the text.

3. Press `Enter`.

The first line moves to the left past the left margin.

TIP: You can apply all the indent options to existing text. Just insert the indent code(s) where you want the indents created.

Centering Text

The old-fashioned way of centering text was to count the number of characters in the text to be entered, subtract that number from the number of characters possible in the line, divide by two, space in that number of spaces, and begin typing. WordPerfect for Windows replaces this tedious operation with the `Shift`+`F7` key combination (or you can select Line and Center from the Layout menu). A code is placed in your text, and the cursor goes to the center of the line. Type in your text. As you type, the characters move to the left or right to even the centering. When you are done, press ⏎Enter. To remove centering, delete the code.

You can also center existing text or multiple lines. Just select the text and press ⇧Shift + F7 (or select Line and Center from the Layout menu). The text in the selection is centered, and the appropriate codes are inserted. The address at the top of the letter shown in Figure 5.7 illustrates several lines that are centered.

Placing Text Flush Right

Figure 5.7 also demonstrates the *Flush Right* option on the date line. You don't have to count characters of text or backspaces; just press Alt + F7, or select Line and Flush Right from the Layout menu. The cursor goes to the right margin. As you type in the text, it aligns with the right margin. Press ⏎Enter to stop typing text that is flush right.

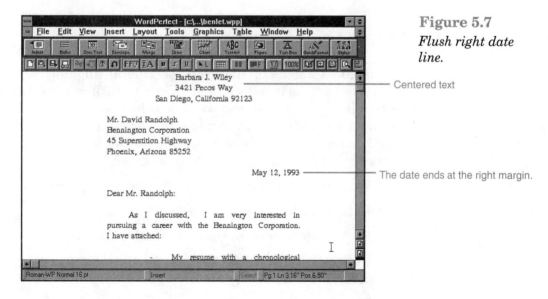

Figure 5.7
Flush right date line.

Centered text

The date ends at the right margin.

To align existing text flush right, place the cursor before the text, and press Alt+F7.

Creating a Pleasing Effect

You can create a pleasing effect by combining tab, indent, center, and flush-right capabilities. For example, you may want the top of a report to have the name of the report indented on the left, the date in the center, and the page number flush right. Just indent, type in the name of the report, center and type in the date, flush right, and enter the page number. The effect might look like this:

Bennington Report   January 10, 1993   Page 6

Later chapters in this book cover how to make such a heading appear on each page of the document, and how to have WordPerfect number pages consecutively for you. For now, just consider how you can combine alignment capabilities for the result you want.

Justifying Text

Justification refers to the even, horizontal alignment of text between margins in a document. When you enter a justification code, all the text that follows it will be justified until a new justification code is entered, or the original one is deleted. WordPerfect's default is called *full justification*, which lines up text evenly between right and left margins.

WordPerfect makes five types of justification possible:

- **Left justification:** Used for most documents.

- **Right justification:** Used for special layouts.

- **Center justification:** Text centered on every line for special layouts.

- **Full justification:** Text aligned evenly between the left and right margins, except for the last line of paragraphs.

- **All** (*full justification, all lines*)**:** Text aligned evenly on left and right margins, including the last line of paragraphs. Some people find this option puts too much white space in the last line of a paragraph.

Figure 5.8 illustrates an advertising piece with each type of justification applied.

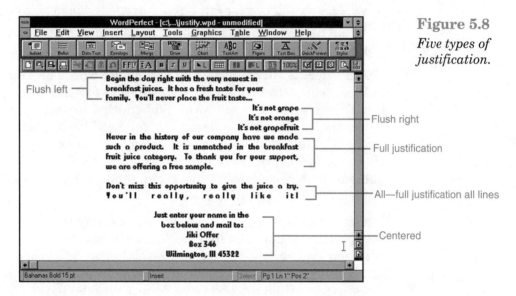

Figure 5.8
Five types of justification.

To justify text follow these steps:

1. Place the insertion point where you want to begin the justification.

2. Select Layout then Justification.

3. Select the type of justification you want. A justification code is placed in your document at the cursor location.

In place of steps 2 and 3 just covered, you may simply position your insertion point and use any one of the following key combinations:

Ctrl+L for Left Justification

Ctrl+R for Right Justification

Ctrl+E for Center Justification

Ctrl+J for Full Justification

To remove or change the justification, delete the first code or enter the code for another type of justification.

If you like the look of full justification, you may want to hyphenate words at the ends of lines to make the lines appear more uniform.

WordPerfect is smart enough to hyphenate words for you automatically. To turn on the hyphenation feature, position the cursor where you want hyphenation to begin. Select the Layout menu, then Line, followed by Hyphenation. On the Line Hyphenation dialog box, check the Hyphenation On check box, and select OK. As you enter and edit text, WordPerfect will prompt you when it needs some help in hyphenating a word.

You can also type hyphens manually. One way is to use the - (minus) key. The hyphen will be in place even if you edit your document—though it may no longer be at the end of a line. This is not good. A preferable course is to use a *soft hyphen* (like the one WordPerfect inserts) that will disappear when the word is no longer at the end of a line. To do this, hold down Ctrl+⇧Shift and press - (the hyphen key). The hyphen only appears on your screen when the word is at the end of a line. A code like this is placed in your document **- Soft Hyphen**.

Showing Symbols

Many symbols can be shown on your screen. For example, you may want to see where you use a space, hard return, tab, indent, center, flush right, and so on. To display symbols, select Show from the View menu. To get rid of the symbols, just select Show again to remove the check mark.

To identify the symbols that appear when you use Show, select Preferences from the File menu. Select the Display icon. On the Display Preferences dialog box, select Show. Check the symbols you want to display. To display the symbols on new documents as well as your current document, check Show Symbols on New and Current Document. (You can deselect Show through the View menu anytime.)

Controlling Line Spacing

Line spacing refers to the number of blank lines between each printed line. The default is single spacing. However, you can double- or triple-space, or space by any number of lines you want to enter. For fine detail in your layouts, you even can enter fractions of a line in the setting. The following Quick Steps detail how to set line spacing.

Setting Line Spacing

1. Select Line, then Spacing, from the Layout menu.

   The Line Spacing dialog box appears.

2. Select Spacing, and enter the number of lines.

   The page visual changes as you change the spacing.

3. Select OK to return to your document.

   A code like this is placed in the document: **Ln Spacing:1.20**. The text following the inserted code follows the new line spacing setting.

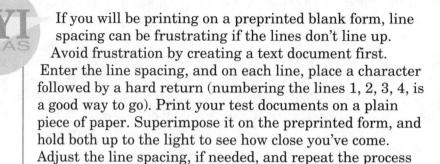

If you will be printing on a preprinted blank form, line spacing can be frustrating if the lines don't line up. Avoid frustration by creating a text document first. Enter the line spacing, and on each line, place a character followed by a hard return (numbering the lines 1, 2, 3, 4, is a good way to go). Print your test documents on a plain piece of paper. Superimpose it on the preprinted form, and hold both up to the light to see how close you've come. Adjust the line spacing, if needed, and repeat the process until you see that the lines will match.

Initial Codes Style

When you looked at the codes in your documents, you may have noticed one that got there all by itself and cannot be deleted. That code is **Open Style:InitialStyle**. This code stands for the defaults for a document, which you can change. For example, you may want to change WordPerfect's default of single-line spacing. If you typically use double spacing, you may get tired of having to set the line spacing for each document. You can change this format (and others) through the *Initial Codes Style* option.

To set the Initial Code Style, follow these steps:

1. Select Document, then Initial Codes Style, from the Layout menu. The Styles Editor appears.

2. On the Styles Editor dialog box, enter any formatting you like in the Contents text area, as the new default(s). You can also delete or edit existing codes.

3. Save the entries by selecting OK.

TIP: To change Initial Codes Style, you must use the **L**ayout menu, **D**ocument, and Initial Codes **S**tyles to reenter the Styles Editor. Make the changes.

TIP: Any codes you enter directly in the body of a document take precedence over the Initial Codes Style. If a file is inserted into another document, the initial codes for the inserted file are inserted along with it.

Change Any Font Settings

1. Press F9, or select the Font from the Layout menu.
2. Select from these options: Font Face, Font Size, Font Style, Appearance, Position, Relative Size, Underline Options, and Color Options.

Change the Initial Font for All New Documents

1. Choose Select Printer from the File menu.
2. Make sure your printer is highlighted, then choose Initial Font.
3. Select the Font Face, Font Size, and Font Style, then choose OK.

Change the Font for a Document

1. Select Document from the Layout menu.
2. Select Initial Font.
3. Select the Font Face, Font Size, and Font Style, then choose OK twice.

Change the Font for Part of a Document

1. Press F9, or select Font from the Layout menu.
2. Select the font settings, then choose OK.

Use QuickFormat

1. With the insertion point in the paragraph, select QuickFormat from the Layout menu.
2. Choose the QuickFormat settings then OK.
3. Select the text to be affected.

Giving Characters a New Look

Changing the look of your characters can add emphasis, interest, and clarity to your documents. The character enhancements possible—and available—depend not only on WordPerfect for Windows, but on your printer. Not all printers are capable of printing all of WordPerfect's character options. You can experiment with your printer to see which results are possible.

WordPerfect's **F**ont command controls the look of your characters. With the **F**ont options, you can control font face, font size, placement, and appearance of characters. Figure 6.1 shows some of these options.

This chapter will explain the various options available, and will provide tips for using character attributes effectively.

Figure 6.1

*Some effects you can create through the **F**ont command.*

Bold:	Bold can **emphasize**.
Underline:	Underline can add <u>interest.</u>
Double Underline:	Double underline can add <u>even more interest.</u>
Redline:	~~Redline~~ text can set off text.
Strikeout:	~~Strikeout~~ does the same.
Shadow:	Shadow is another look.
Small Caps	SMALL CAPS gives this appearance.
Superscript:	Use superscript in footnotes.[2]
Subscript:	Subscript is good for text like H_2O.
Fine:	Fine text is one size.
Large:	Large is another
Extra Large	Extra large is another.
Some type styles:	Helvetica, Roman, Courier

Fonts

Your printer has specific typeface and size capabilities. On many printers, it is possible to print in more than one typeface, and in more than one size. For example, Figure 6.2 shows a sample résumé, printed with the headings in a large Helvetica typeface and the body in a smaller Roman typeface.

NOTE: *Typeface* refers to the general family of the letters. Helvetica is an example of a typeface; Times Roman is another. (This book is printed in New Baskerville.)

Text in a particular typeface can appear in a variety of *sizes*, from about 6 points (6/72 of an inch) to as high as 70 points or more, depending on the printer's capabilities.

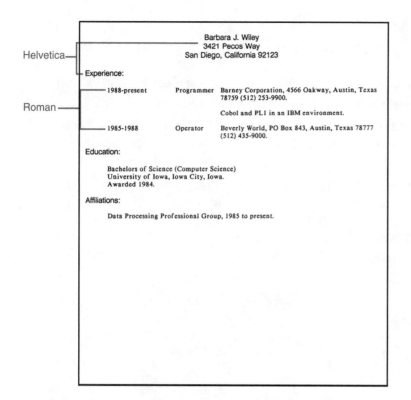

Figure 6.2

A résumé with Helvetica and Roman fonts.

WordPerfect for Windows offers several ways to control fonts. Each method allows you to choose from the same list of fonts—which in turn is determined by the fonts available to your particular printer.

Setting the Initial Font for All Documents

An *initial font* can be set up to be the default for all documents you create when a given printer is selected. This font is used unless you specify another font (using one of the methods discussed later in this chapter). To change the initial font (in the printer file), follow these Quick Steps.

QUICK STEPS

Setting the Printer Initial Font

1. Choose Select Printer from the File menu.

   The Select Printer dialog box appears.

2. Make sure your printer is selected, then choose Initial Font.

   The Printer Initial Font dialog box appears (see Figure 6.3).

3. Select the Font Face, Font Size, and Font Style, then select OK, followed by Close.

   The initial font for all documents is set.

Figure 6.3

Printer Initial Font dialog box.

Setting the Document Initial Font

If you want to use a different font for one document, you need not change the initial font for all documents. You can set the *document initial font*. The document initial font setting is valid for the active document only, and overrides the default font. To set the Initial Font for the document, use these Quick Steps.

Setting the Document Initial Font

1. Choose Document from the Layout menu, then Initial Font.

   The Document Initial Font dialog box appears (see Figure 6.4).

2. Select the Font Face, Font Size, and Font Style.

   The initial font for the document is identified.

3. Select OK to return to your document.

   The initial font for the current document is set.

For example, in Figure 6.4, the words "The Quick" appear in the Frankenstein font face, size 46, and regular style. It's a nice setting for a Haunted House party flyer.

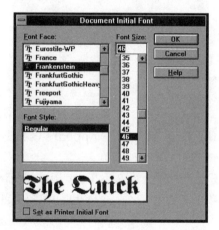

Figure 6.4

The Document Initial Font dialog box.

Changing the Font Within a Document

You're not limited to one font in a document; you can use as many fonts as your printer supports, changing as often as you want. Just use the Font option, which overrides any fonts set through the other methods. It inserts a font code at the beginning and end of the selected text, just as when you select a size or appearance (as you will see later in the chapter). Alternatively, a code goes into the document at the insertion point, and affects all text which follows. You can use Reveal Codes (Alt + F3) to see the codes.

To change the font, use the following Quick Steps.

Changing the Font Within a Document

1. Place the insertion point where the font is to change. (All text from the insertion point forward will be affected.)

   or

   Select the text to be changed. (Only the selected text will be affected.)

2. Press F9 , or select Font from the Layout menu. | The Font dialog box appears (see Figure 6.5).

3. Select the Font Face, Font Size, and Font Style. | Text illustrating your selections appears.

4. Select OK twice. | You are returned to your document. The font is the new default for the document.

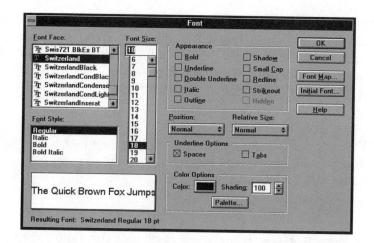

Figure 6.5
The Font dialog box.

When you choose a font (using any of the methods we've discussed), you are defining a combination of font face, size, and style to be the normal font for your document. Once you have defined what is "normal," you can concentrate on creating variations to make your document more interesting.

Controlling the Relative Size of Characters

No matter how carefully you choose your font, at times you will want to make certain words larger or smaller. WordPerfect offers several options for changing the size of text for emphasis, aesthetic appeal, or simply to fit more text on a page.

Font size is measured in *points*. There are 72 points in an inch. When you change font size, you change from one point size to another.

In contrast, when you change the *Relative Size* of text, you don't specify a point size; you specify, in words, how you want the size to change. For example, you might specify very large. When you do this, WordPerfect examines the size of the currently selected font, and multiplies its size by a fixed percentage to determine how big "very large" would be in comparison to it. You can use the following words to change the size: Fine, Small, Normal, Large, Very Large, and Extra Large.

TIP: Some fonts are *scalable*—their size can be controlled with the Relative Size feature. Not all printers support scalable fonts.

To assign a size to existing text, use the following Quick Steps.

Selecting Font Size for Existing Text

1. Use F8 or the mouse to select the text you want to alter.

   The text is highlighted.

2. Press F9, or select Font from the Layout menu.

   The Font dialog box appears.

3. Select the Relative Size you want, and select OK.

   Codes reflecting your selection are placed in your document on either side of the selected text.

To change the size of text you are about to type, follow these next Quick Steps.

Selecting Font Size for New Text

1. Press F9, or select Font from the Layout menu.

   The Font dialog box appears.

2. Select the Relative Size you want, and select OK.

   Codes reflecting your selection are placed in your document on either side of the insertion point.

To stop using the Relative Size, use the → key to move past the end code for the Relative Size. Figure 6.6 shows the various sizes available, as well as examples of superscript and subscript (covered in the next section).

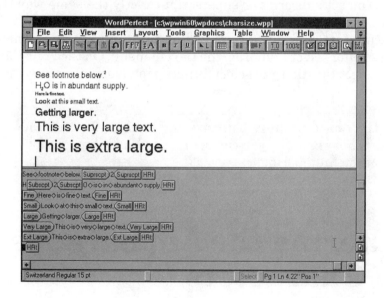

Figure 6.6
Relative Size and Position attributes in both the document and Reveal Codes screen.

Controlling Character Position

In some instances, you may want characters to appear slightly above or below the normal line of text. WordPerfect for Windows offers two common options for positioning text:

Superscript: Superscript characters are placed somewhat above the line of normal text. Text in superscript is often used for footnotes and formulas. Most printers are capable of printing superscript text.

Subscript: Subscript characters are placed slightly lower than the line of text. Formulas often require subscripted text. Common printers can handle this option.

You set subscript or superscript exactly the same way that you set size (see the preceding section). You can either set it for existing text or for new text, just as you can with size. Briefly, press F9 or select Font from the Layout menu. On the Font dialog box, select Position and select Superscript, Normal, or Subscript.

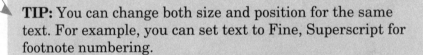

TIP: You can change both size and position for the same text. For example, you can set text to Fine, Superscript for footnote numbering.

Altering the Appearance of Characters

NOTE: *Appearance*, as WordPerfect uses it, means the presence or absence of attributes such as bold, italic, underline, redline, and strikeout.

WordPerfect's Appearance options have something for everyone. Figure 6.7 shows some of the Appearance options you can select. The options available are:

Bold: Bold text is heavier than normal text. Usually, bold text is displayed on-screen as brighter than other text, or in a different color.

Underline: Text may be printed with a single underline. For underlines to be continuous across spaces or between Tabs, in the Underline Options select Spaces and/or Tabs. Select neither, and underlining will stop at spaces and tabs.

Double underline: Text may be printed with two underlines. Some printers do not handle this option. If your printer does, it can give your documents an unusual touch.

Italic: If your printer handles italic text, you can introduce a typeset quality to your documents. Use it sparingly to emphasize key words or phrases. Use it throughout invitations or announcements to give them an elegant appearance.

Outline: This special style is useful as an attention-getter, although many printers do not handle the style.

Shadow: This option creates a shadow effect by offsetting a character from itself. Shadow is effective for use in flyers and advertisements.

Small Caps: Regardless of whether you enter the text in upper- or lowercase letters, the text is printed in small uppercase (capital) letters.

Redline: This option is often used to display edits that should be reviewed. Text to be added can be shown in redline.

Strikeout: When showing edits made to a document, you can use strikeout to illustrate text to be removed.

TIP: To set text to color or gray shade, use the Color Options on the Font dialog box. For example, you may create gray by setting the Color to black and the Shading to 50%. Try it out with your printer to see what is supported.

Figure 6.7
Examples of character appearance options.

Normal

Bold

<u>Underline</u>

<u>Double Underline</u>

Italics

Shadow

Small Caps

Redline

~~Strikeout~~

TIP: The Appearances may be selected directly from the Font dialog box. If you are entering a single, commonly-used appearance, however, it may be faster to use a short-cut key. Use Ctrl+B for Bold, Ctrl+U for Underline, and Ctrl+I for Italics.

The following Quick Steps describe the process of changing an Appearance for existing text.

Setting Appearance for Existing Text

1. Use F8 or the mouse to select the text you want to alter.	Text is highlighted.
2. Press F9, or select Font from the Layout menu.	The Font dialog box appears.
3. Place a check in the box of each Appearance desired.	The selected appearances have a check in each box.
4. Select OK.	

Codes are placed in your document before and after the text you have selected. Figure 6.8 illustrates the document and Reveal Codes screen for the Appearances. If you have a color monitor, redline appears in red.

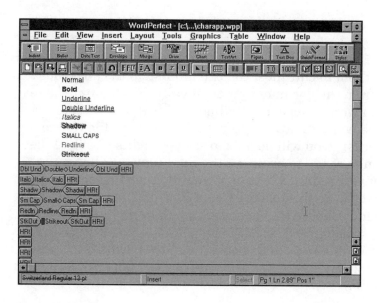

Figure 6.8
Appearances in the document and in Reveal Codes.

To change the Appearances of text you are about to enter, press F9, or select Font from the Layout menu. Check the Appearances you want, and then choose OK. Type the text. To move beyond the ending Appearances code, select a different Appearance, or press the → key.

As with Relative Size choices, you can combine Appearances, or you can combine Relative Size with Appearances. (For example, you can select Very Large Bold Italic text.) Just make the necessary selections.

TIP: With WordPerfect, you can select text and convert it to uppercase, lowercase, or initial caps. (Initial caps changes the first letter in each word to a capital letter.) Select the block of text you want to convert, including the punctuation. Select Convert Case from the Edit menu. Identify whether you want the result in Lowercase, Uppercase, or Initial Caps.

Redline and strikeout have a nifty bonus. When you use them to edit files, you can later strip the strikeout text from the document automatically. First, enter the text you want inserted in redline, and text you want deleted in strikeout. You can then pass a copy of the file to a co-worker, who will be able to see your edits clearly. When you're ready to print out the final copy, you'll want to convert redlined text to normal text, and remove strikeout text. To do this, choose Compare Document from the File menu. Choose Remove Markings. On the Remove Markings dialog box, select Remove Redline markings and Strikeout Text, and choose OK. (If you choose to Remove Strikeout Text Only, the redline markings will still be in place.)

Additional Fonts

If your printer comes with only a few fonts, you're not stuck. There are several ways to get extra fonts to use in WordPerfect for Windows. One method, WordPerfect's fonts, is free; it requires only that your printer be capable of printing graphics. (Nearly all printers except daisywheel models can do this.) Other options are cartridges and fonts you can buy separately from WordPerfect.

WordPerfect's Fonts

WordPerfect for Windows set up its fonts when the printer was selected (as part of the installation procedure); they are available when you press F9 or select Font from the Layout menu. Each font has a different look. When you use the font, the look appears on the Font dialog box. You will want to experiment with your printer to see the printed result.

Font Cartridges and Soft Fonts

Many printers, particularly laser printers, will print additional fonts (combinations of typefaces and sizes). You can purchase these separately as a cartridge that plugs into the printer, or as software you install on your computer (these are called *downloadable* or *soft* fonts).

If you have a cartridge or soft fonts installed, support may already have been set up during the installation of WordPerfect for Windows. If so, soft fonts appear when you use F9 or select Font from the Layout menu.

You may check the installation of cartridges as follows. Select Select Printer from the File menu. On the Select Printer dialog box, make sure your printer is selected. Choose Setup. If your cartridges are set up, they appear in the Cartridges list. Choose (highlight) the cartridges you want available. Some printers limit the number of cartridges you can select.

If the cartridges or soft fonts are not set up, you need to tell WordPerfect what soft fonts and cartridges you want to use. Do this using the following steps:

1. Select Select Printer from the File menu. The Select Printer dialog box appears.

2. Select Setup. Select Cartridges as appropriate for your printer.

3. Select Fonts. The Font Installer dialog box appears.

4. Select Add Fonts. The Add Fonts dialog box appears.

5. Enter the source drive and directory of the soft fonts (or the cartridge's support files), and select OK. The fonts are shown on the right of the Font Installer dialog box.

6. On the list, select the fonts to install. The fonts are selected.

7. Choose the Add Fonts button. The Add Fonts dialog box appears.

8. Enter the destination directory of the fonts, and choose OK (if they are already on the hard disk, keep the same directory as the source directory, or enter the default printer's font directory C:\PCLFONTS).

9. Choose Exit, then OK, followed by Close.

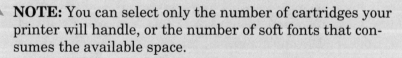

NOTE: You can select only the number of cartridges your printer will handle, or the number of soft fonts that consumes the available space.

The steps given here are the basic ones for selecting a cartridge or soft font for use. Dealing with cartridges and soft fonts can become very complex. If you run into trouble, consult your WordPerfect Reference or a more advanced book.

Using QuickFormat

QuickFormat can be used to save time when you format text to match existing formats. To use QuickFormat, place the insertion point in a paragraph that contains the format you wish to copy to other existing text. Select **QuickFormat** from the Layout menu. The QuickFormat dialog box shown in Figure 6.9 appears. Identify whether you want to capture the Fonts and Attributes, Paragraph Styles, or Both. Select OK. The mouse pointer appears as a paint brush. Use it to select the text to which the format should be applied. Figure 6.10 shows text in a script selected with the special pointer. Once the text is selected and you release the left mouse button, the format is applied. To turn off QuickFormat, select QuickFormat again from the Layout menu, or simply type a character.

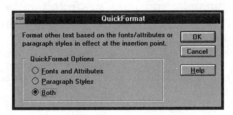

Figure 6.9
The QuickFormat dialog box.

Figure 6.10

The text selected to apply the QuickFormat.

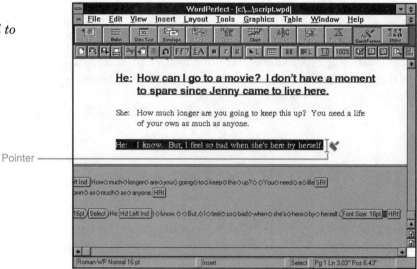

Pointer

WordPerfect Characters

WordPerfect Characters are characters and graphic symbols that are not available on your keyboard. You can print out these special characters if you have a graphics printer, or if you have a font that contains the characters.

WordPerfect Characters include characters as diverse as pointing fingers, pencils, and diacritics for phonetic values such as accent e (é), and tilde n (ñ). To use one of the available characters, follow these Quick Steps:

Inserting a WordPerfect Character

1. Position your insertion point where you want the character to appear, and press Ctrl+W, or select Character from the Insert menu.

The WordPerfect Characters dialog box appears.

2. Select the Character Set containing the character you want.	The characters appear.
3. Select the Character from those that appear, or type in the Number assigned to the character.	The character is identified.
4. Select Insert and Close.	The symbol appears in your document at the insertion point.

Special Characters include ANSI characters and IBM PC Extended Characters such as boxes, lines, and other symbols. To use characters from either group, simply hold down Alt while typing the corresponding number on the numeric keypad (*not* the numbers across the top of your computer keyboard). Release Alt.

CAUTION

Not all graphic displays will show all the characters possible through WordPerfect. Not all printers will print each character. Experiment with your display and printer to see what capabilities are available.

Bullets and Numbers

You may also insert bullets and numbers to set off the start of a paragraph. Place your insertion point in the paragraph which the bullet or number should precede. Select Bullets & Numbers from the Insert menu. On the Bullets & Numbers dialog box, select the bullet or number you want, then select OK. The bullet or number will appear at the start of the paragraph, indenting is added, and codes are placed in your document. (You may also press Ctrl+Shift+B to insert the default bullet, or use the Bullet button on the Button Bar.)

Select the Printer File to Use

1. Select Print from the File menu, or press F5.
2. Choose Select to change the printer chosen.
3. Highlight a printer on the Select Printer dialog box, and choose Select.

Print a Document

1. Select Print from the File menu, or press F5.
2. Identify what you want to print (such as Full Document or Current Page).
3. Select any other options, such as the Number of Copies.
4. Select Print.

Printing Part of a Document

1. Select the text to print.
2. Select Print from the File menu, or press F5.
3. Enter the number of copies and select Print.

Printing a Document on Disk

1. Select Print from the File menu, or press F5.
2. Select Document on Disk, then Print.
3. Enter the Filename and Page(s) if needed, then select Print.

Printing Multiple Documents on Disk

1. Press F5, or select Print from the File menu.
2. Select Document on Disk, then Print.
3. Choose the list button at the right of the Filename text box.
4. Highlight each document to print.
5. Select the Options button, then choose Print from the drop-down list.

Chapter 7

Printing Your Work

For most WordPerfect users, printing is the reason for all the rest of the work—getting a paper copy to be mailed or presented. This chapter covers what you need to know to identify your printer to WordPerfect, and print all (or part) of a document.

Setting Up Your Printer

When you installed Windows, you identified the brand and type of printer you use. There are additional setup steps you can perform from within WordPerfect that help identify the printer.

Press F5, or select Print from the File menu. The Print dialog box (shown in Figure 7.1) appears. The currently-selected printer is listed. If you are using only one printer, and are not printing any fancy special effects, all you need do is make sure the name of the printer appears here.

If you installed more than one printer and need to change the printer selected—or if you need to set up options for fancy printing jobs (for example, using special fonts loaded from a disk)—choose the Select button on the Print dialog box. This displays the Select Printer dialog box, which shows you the printers you have installed.

Figure 7.1
The Print dialog box.

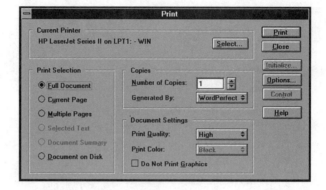

Among the options available from the Select Printer dialog box are:

- **S**elect: To select the printer which is highlighted in the list.

- **S**etup: To identify setup options for the printer, such as the **R**esolution, Paper Si**z**e, Paper **S**ource, and so on.

- **A**dd Printer: To select other printer files that were installed. (See Appendix B for installation instructions.)

Once you have highlighted the printer you want and chosen the **S**elect button, you are returned to the Print dialog box. Choose Close to return to WordPerfect for Windows.

Printing a Document

Once you have selected the appropriate printer, make sure your printer is ready to print:

- Is the cable between the printer and computer secure on both ends?

- Is the printer turned on? If not, make sure it is plugged in, and then turn it on.

- Is the *on-line* light lit? If not, use the panel to put the printer on-line (which means it is ready to receive your document from the computer).

- Is there paper in the printer, and is it fed properly? If not, add paper, and make sure it feeds smoothly into the printer.

When your printer is ready and the document you want to print is showing on your screen, press F5, or select Print from the File menu. The Print dialog box (shown in Figure 7.1) appears.

To print the entire document, select Full Document. To print only the page on which your insertion point rests, select Current Page. (To print certain pages, select Multiple Pages. The Multiple Pages print option is covered in detail in Chapter 9.)

To print more than one paper copy, select Number of Copies, and type in the number of copies you want. Typically, you will want copies Generated by WordPerfect, rather than sending the copies to the printer and having them generated in a different sort order. For example, if you are printing two copies of a three-page document, WordPerfect will print pages 1 through 3 of one document, then print the next documents (also in numerical order). If the print is generated by the printer, two copies of page 1 may print, followed by two copies of page 2 and so on.

The Print dialog box also allows you to set the Print Quality and Print Color (if you have a color printer). Finally, if you want to skip the graphics (and save time during the print), check Do Not Print Graphics.

Select the Options button on the Print dialog box to meet special printing needs. The following options become available on the Print Output Options dialog box. Make any selections you desire, then choose OK to return to the Print dialog box.

- Print Document Summary: Select this option to print a summary of your document when the document is printed.

- **B**ooklet Printing: To arrange pages if you subdivide the page (see your WordPerfect for Windows manual for more information).

- Print in **R**everse Order (Back to Front): Prints pages from the last page to the first page.

- Print **O**dd/Even Pages: To print only odd- or even-numbered pages. This is useful if your printer doesn't handle two-sided printing automatically. Print all odd pages, turn over the pages and load the printer, then print the even pages.

- Output Bin Options: If your printer has multiple bins for paper coming out of the printer, you can identify how the paper is output.

NOTE: To print only selected text, choose Selected Text. To print a document that is on disk (not on your screen), select Document on Disk. Both options are discussed in detail later in this chapter.

The following Quick Steps explain how to print a document.

Print a Document

1. With the document on the screen, press [F5], or select Print from the File menu.

   The Print dialog box appears.

2. Select Full Document to print the entire document, or Current Page to print the page the insertion point is on.

   The Print setting is complete.

3. Select Number of Copies and enter a number, if you want more than one copy.

   The number of copies appears.

4. Identify the Print Quality and Print Color; check Do Not Print Graphics if you want to save print time.	The Document settings are complete.
5. If you have special print output needs, select the Options button and complete the selections. Choose OK.	You are on the Print dialog box.
6. Select Print.	The document prints.

Printing on Different Paper Sizes and Types

You may have more than one size or type of paper in a document. For example, you may have a letter to be printed on 8.5-by-11-inch paper, followed by text to be printed on an envelope. In such a case, put the different paper sizes or types on different pages, and print each page separately (by using F5, and then Current Page). This will give you time to hand-feed the paper to the printer, or change the paper that is automatically fed through the printer.

Printing a Selected Part of a Document

In the previous section, you saw how to print a single page. But what if you want to print a few paragraphs, but not the entire page? Or a range of paragraphs that begins halfway down a page and ends halfway down another page?

Select the text you want to print. Press F5 or select Print from the File menu. This sets Print Selection in the Print dialog box automatically for Selected Text. Enter the Number of Copies, and select Print.

Printing One or More Documents on Disk

You may want to print one or more documents that are on a disk (not appearing in a window). To print one document, follow these steps:

Print a Document on Disk

1. Press F5, or select Print from the File menu.

   The Print dialog box appears.

2. Select Document on Disk, then Print.

   The Document on Disk dialog box (shown in Figure 7.2) appears.

3. Enter or select the Filename of the file you want to print, and identify the pages to print. Then select Print.

   The document is printed.

Figure 7.2

The Document on Disk dialog box.

Button to list and select multiple files to print

Document on Disk

Document
Filename: c:\wpwin60\wpdocs\ben
Page(s): all
Secondary Page(s):
Chapter(s):
Volume(s):

Print
Cancel
Help

TIP: When you identify pages to print, you may identify consecutive pages with a hyphen and non-consecutive pages with a comma. For example, to print pages 1 through 4 and page 6, enter 1-4, 6 (always enter the pages in numerical order). More information about printing multiple copies is in Chapter 9.

If you want to print multiple files, press F5, or select Print from the File menu. Select Document on Disk, then Print. On the Document on Disk dialog box, choose the button right of the Filename text box to list and select files. The Select File dialog box (shown in Figure 7.3) will appear. Select (highlight) each file in the list that you want to print. Then select the File Options button. In the drop-down list which appears, choose Print. Each file you selected is printed.

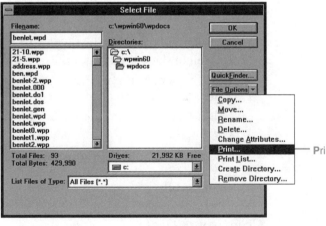

Figure 7.3
The Select File dialog box.

Print on the File Options drop-down list

Displaying the Ruler Bar

1. Press Alt+⇧Shift+F3, or select Ruler Bar from the View menu.

Entering Tabs

1. Select Line from the Layout menu.
2. Select Tab Set.
3. On the Tab Set dialog box, enter the Settings, Position From, and Dot Leader Options.
   OR
1. Use the Tab Set button on the Power Bar to select the type of tab.
2. Click on the Ruler Bar to set a tab; drag a tab to relocate; or drag a tab off the bar to delete.

Using Columns

1. Select Columns from the Layout menu.
2. Complete the definitions, and select OK.
3. Enter text in columns. Press Ctrl+⏎Enter to start a new column or to end a series of columns.
4. Select Columns from the Layout menu, then Off.
   OR
1. Use the Columns Define button on the Power Bar to define columns, break a column, and turn columns off.

Creating a Table

1. Select Table, and then Create.
2. Enter the number of columns and rows, and select OK.
3. Select Table, then use the editing and formula command options.

8

Using Tabs, Columns, and Tables

Arranging text on the screen can be streamlined with the use of tabs, columns, and tables. This chapter not only covers how to change WordPerfect's default tab settings, but also how to add a variety of tabs specific to your needs. In addition, you will learn how to create columns and tables; this procedure can simplify working with text you want to keep together in columns (or columns and rows).

The Ruler Bar and Power Bar

Display the *Ruler Bar* to identify current margin and tab settings, and to change them.

The sample résumé in Figure 8.1 is shown with the Ruler Bar displayed. On it, you can see current tab settings (denoted by triangles) and margins. Figure 8.1 also shows the button on the

Power Bar which is handy to use with the Ruler Bar when you add tab settings. To display the Ruler Bar, select View, Ruler Bar (or press Alt + ⇧Shift + F3). When Ruler Bar is checked on the View menu, it is displayed. To remove the display of the Ruler Bar, just select View, Ruler Bar (or press Alt + ⇧Shift + F3 again).

Figure 8.1

Use the Power Bar's Tab Set button to set tabs on the Ruler Bar.

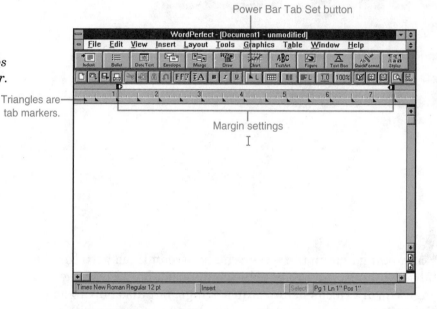

Power Bar Tab Set button

Triangles are tab markers.

Margin settings

Default Tabs

A tab in WordPerfect for Windows is like a tab setting on a typewriter, only better. At the basic level, you press Tab⇄ to indent the first line of a paragraph, or select F7 to indent the entire paragraph. The insertion point moves to the next column marked by a tab setting, and a **Left Tab** or **Hd Left Ind** code appears in your text. At a more sophisticated level, according to the type of tab setting you enter, you can align characters on the left, on the right, by any character, or you can center the characters.

The tabs shown in Figure 8.1 are the default tabs. WordPerfect for Windows comes with default tab settings every half inch. Notice that with the default tab settings, you have to press F7 several times to complete the entries. As you'll learn later in this chapter, you can specify new tab settings anywhere you like. By entering your own tab settings, you can reduce the number of times you have to press [Tab⁵] or [F7].

> **TIP:** Use tabs for aligning single-line text. If you often want text to wrap around within a column for easier entry and editing, try the *parallel column* feature or tables. Both are discussed later in this chapter.

Tab Types and Settings

WordPerfect uses four basic types of tabs (each with a variation covered later):

- Left
- Decimal
- Center
- Right

In Figure 8.2, the fund-raising activities included on the résumé illustrate each type of tab setting. A description of each type follows.

Left Tab

The *left tab* setting is the default WordPerfect uses. When you use a left tab setting and begin typing, the text is entered one space to the right of the tab setting. The **Left Tab** code is placed in your text. In Figure 8.2, the titles (such as Committee Chair) are aligned under the standard left tab setting.

Figure 8.2

Types of tab settings.

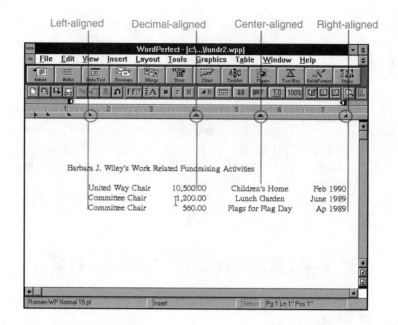

Decimal Tab

You set a *decimal tab* to align text (usually dollar amounts) on a decimal point. When you press [Tab ⁑], the **Dec Tab** code is entered into the text. Text you type in is entered to the left of the decimal tab until you press the decimal point (a period). Then the text is entered to the right. This feature is especially helpful when you want to enter columns of financial figures, as in Figure 8.2, where the money raised is aligned under the decimal point.

Center Tab

The *center tab* is used to center text under the tab setting automatically, as you type. Setting a center tab enables you to enter text before and after the centered text on the line, as shown in Figure 8.2. You can also see that the **Center Tab** code is entered into the text.

Right Tab

The *right tab* setting is used to align text on a rightmost character. As you enter text, it moves left until you finish typing. The code **Right Tab** appears in the text. In Figure 8.2, the year is entered using the right tab setting, which makes an even right margin. You can, however, place the right tab setting anywhere in a line.

To use each of these tab settings, you don't need to press special keys—just the standard Tab⇥ key. You do, however, need to set tab settings to tell WordPerfect where to place the tabs, and what type of tab setting to use.

> **TIP:** You can enter a specific type of tab for one time only as a *hard tab*. For example, you might want a right tab at the next tab setting only (without changing the tab settings for the whole document). The tabs can be entered with or without *dot leaders*, a series of characters (usually dots) between tabs. To enter a hard tab, position your insertion point where you want the tab to appear. Select Layout, Line, then Other Codes. On the Other Codes dialog box, identify the Hard Tab Codes or Hard Tab Codes with Dot Leaders you want. Select Insert.

Changing Tab Settings

You can set up WordPerfect for Windows to use any of the four types of tabs. First, however, you need to decide where you want tab settings placed. To determine an exact location, just measure your page, and identify the location of the tab settings: from the left edge of the page for *Absolute* tab settings, or from the left margin for *Relative* tab settings. For example, specifying an Absolute tab setting at 3" means the tab setting will be 3 inches from the left edge of the paper, not 3 inches from the left margin setting. You may also just eyeball the tab locations and begin entering new tab settings; you will have to visualize their effects on the document as you work.

Becoming familiar with how to set tabs offers several benefits:

- You can use all four types of tabs, instead of being stuck with left tabs only.

- By setting your own tabs, you can reduce the number of times you have to press ⎡Tab⁺⎤ or ⎡F7⎤.

- You can use tabs to change the layout of your text easily. Simply entering new tab settings will rearrange the text after those tab settings.

The following Quick Steps detail how to set tabs.

Manipulating Tabs Using Bars

1. To add a tab, select the Tab Set button in the Power Bar; on the menu that appears, select the type of tab desired, and make sure Set Tabs is checked.

   The symbol for the type of tab you have chosen appears in the button.

2. Using the mouse, click on the Ruler Bar in the location at which you want the tab.

   The tab appears.

3. To move the tab, just drag it to the new location.

   The tab is relocated.

4. To delete a tab, just drag it off the Ruler Bar.

   The tab is deleted.

When you select the Tab Set button on the Power Bar, you can also clear all tabs by making that selection. (Another hint: instead of using the Tab Set button on the Power Bar, you can click the right mouse button on the lower portion of the Ruler Bar to open the Quick Menu. Tab options appear on the Quick Menu.)

TIP: You may move left and right margin settings on the Ruler Bar. Just drag the left and right margin symbols to the location desired.

For finer control of tabs (or if you don't like to use the mouse), you may also set, move, and delete tabs using the menu. Select Layout, Line, Tab Set (alternatively, double-click on the lower portion of the Ruler Bar. The Tab Set dialog box appears (see Figure 8.3). Here you may identify the Type of tab setting from the drop-down list, and its Position in decimals. If you want the tab to repeat, enter a value for Repeat Every (you may need to clear all tabs first with the Clear All button). Next, identify whether your position is from the Left Margin or Left Edge of Paper. Complete these settings for a tab, then select Set. (If you are clearing an existing tab, identify the information and select Clear.) When all tabs are set, select OK.

Any time you want to "start from scratch", you can. On the Tab Set dialog box, you may remove all tabs by selecting the Clear All button, or reset the tabs to default with the Default button.

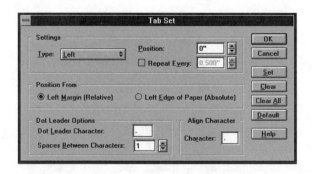

Figure 8.3
The Tab Set dialog box.

You may want to try out a new tab setting for existing text without deleting or changing the existing tab setting. That way, if you don't like the new setting, you can delete the code and still have the old tab setting. Be careful. If you place your insertion point just after the existing tab setting code, and then set up the new code, the existing tab setting code will simply be edited; you will have lost the old tab settings. Instead, enter a hard return (by pressing ⏎Enter)), or enter some text after the old tab setting. Enter your new setting. Both codes will exist in your text, and you will be able to change your mind and delete either code.

Dot Leaders

Occasionally, you may want to enter a row of dots (called *dot leaders*) between items of text at tab settings. In Figure 8.4, dot leaders have been added to some of the tab settings (along with a new font).

Figure 8.4

Dot leaders added to the text along with a new font.

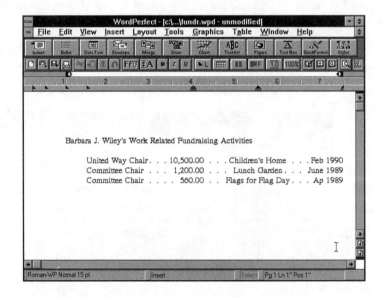

> **TIP:** You can mix dot-leader tabs with other tabs set in the same tab setting. They all appear on the Ruler Bar at once.

To enter a tab setting to include dot leaders, use the same methods to enter regular tabs. From the type of tabs you'll select from, just identify a dot-leader tab. Adding dot leaders does not affect existing tabs.

You can change the character used for dot leaders, or change the amount of space between characters in a dot leader. To do this, go to the Tab Set dialog box via Layout, Line, Tab Set. Or right-click on the lower portion of the Ruler Bar to use the Quick Menu to select Tab Set. On the Tab Set dialog box, look at the Dot Leader Options. After Dot Leader Character, type in any keyboard character. In Spaces **B**etween Characters, enter the number of spaces that will appear between each dot-leader character.

Entering Tabbed Headings

When you use tab settings, often you are creating columns of text for which you want headings. You will want the headings to be aligned over the columns in most cases, rather than aligned the same way as the tabular data beneath them. If this is the case, you have several options:

- You can place your headings before the tab code (so that the earlier tab settings are used, if they are more appropriate than the newer ones).

- You can type in the headings, using spaces instead of tabs.

- You can create a set of tab settings especially for the headings, and create another set for the data after the headings are typed.

Of these three methods, the last is probably the most reliable, since creating new tab settings especially for the headings, will make them exactly the way you want them.

CAUTION   If you choose to use spaces rather than tabs, be aware that some printers do not measure the spaces between tab settings and the spaces entered with the Spacebar in the same way. Thus, your headings can appear lined up on the screen, but not when printed. You may need to experiment with your printer to get the outcome you want.

Changing the Decimal Align Character

The default *decimal align character* used with the Decimal Tab is a period (.). When you use decimal tab settings, you type in a period as the alignment character, and the text lines up according to the period. You can align by any character, however—not just a period. For example, you might want to align text on an equals sign (=) as shown next:

        6+9+4=19
         8+2=10

    800+310=1110

To change the decimal align character, make sure your insertion point is above the tabs you want to affect, and follow these Quick Steps:

Changing the Decimal Align Character

1. Select Layout, Line, Tab Set, or click the right mouse button on the lower portion of the Ruler Bar and select Tab Set from the Quick Menu.

   The Tab Set dialog box appears.

2. Type in the character you want to use in the Character text box under Align Character.

   The new align character appears.

3. Select OK, and return to your document.

   A code like this appears in your document, identifying the decimal/align character: **Dec/Align Char:=**.

The character after **Char:** is the new decimal align character; it will be used in text entered after the code. In this example, it is the equals sign. You can restore the period as the decimal align character at any time by deleting the code, or by specifying a period as the new decimal align character.

Columns

WordPerfect's *Columns* feature is useful if you want to create any type of document with two to twenty-four columns on a page. Scripts, newsletters, and lists are popular applications.

The following are the types of columns shown in Figures 8.5a and 8.5b:

Figure 8.5a
Newspaper columns.

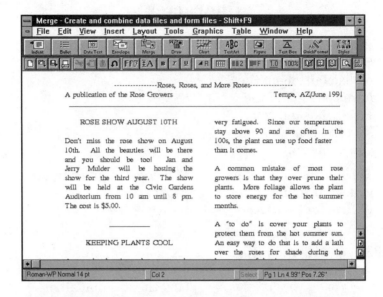

Figure 8.5b
Parallel columns.

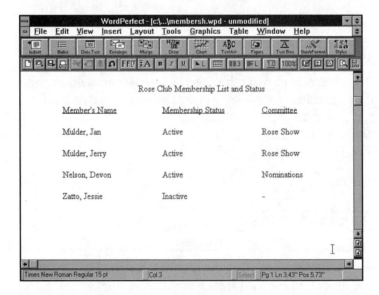

- **Newspaper** (balanced or not): Text flows from the bottom of one column to the top of the next (good for newsletters). If you choose to use Balanced Newspaper Columns, each column is adjusted to be equal in length on the page.

- **Parallel** (with or without block protect): Text is grouped across the page in rows. Related text across columns can be Block Protected to stay together on a page (good for lists where the text in each line relates).

Notice that the beginning text in Figure 8.5a is not in column format, and provides the heading for our newsletter.

To get started, you must define the columns you want to use. To do this, follow these next Quick Steps. Start with the insertion point where you want the column to begin. Or select a block of text to place in the columns.

Defining Columns

1. Select Columns, then Define from the Layout menu.

   The Columns dialog box (shown in Figure 8.6) appears.

2. Under Number of Columns, enter the Columns you want on the page.

   The number you enter appears.

3. Choose the type of column you want (Newspaper, Balanced Newspaper, Parallel, or Parallel w/Block Protect).

   The type you select is marked.

4. If you want to control the space between columns and rows, enter values for Spacing Between Columns and Spacing Between Rows in Parallel Columns.

   The distances between columns and rows appear.

continues

continued

5. Enter the width of each column under Column Widths (especially if columns have different widths).

The column widths are set.

6. Choose OK, and return to your document to begin entering text in the columns.

The **Col Def** code appears in your document. You can begin typing in columns.

Figure 8.6
The Columns dialog box.

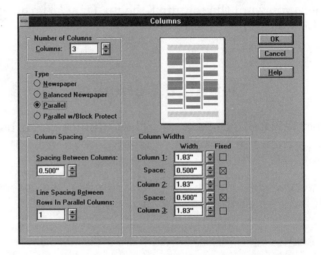

CAUTION When you enter the width and distance between columns, make sure your numbers match. For example, there can't be two evenly spaced columns that are 4 inches wide, each with a 1-inch space between columns, on an 8.5-by-11-inch page. Such a request calls for more width than is available on the page; 4 + 4 + 1 equals 9 inches, not 8.5.

Turning Columns Off and On

Once you have entered text in a column, you may want to turn columns off, enter text, and then turn columns back on. For example, this is helpful if you want to enter a heading horizontally across several columns and then return to using columns. To turn columns off, choose Columns from the Layout menu, then select Off. You are returned to your document where a column code is inserted.

To turn columns back on, you can copy the column code and border code (if any) to the location where you want columns to start up again.

If you are using five or fewer columns, and can use default WordPerfect settings, there is a faster way to control columns. Use the Power Bar. Place the insertion point where you want the columns to start (or select the text for the columns). Click on the Columns Define button, and select the number of columns (2 Columns through 5 Columns). You may also use the Columns Define Power Bar button to select Columns Off, select Define to go to the Columns dialog box, or select Column Break to end one column and start another.

Working with Text in Columns

To enter text in a column, begin typing after the column definition code. You can use any typical editing features in columns, along with fonts, graphics, and other effects.

Starting a new column is easy. The method is the same for Newspaper (not balanced) and Parallel Column (with or without Block Protect). When you want to begin a new column, press Ctrl+⏎Enter to create a hard column break (or select Column Break on the Columns Define Power Bar button). You go to the next column, and a Hard Column Break code **[HCol]** is placed in your document. Figure 8.7 illustrates how the text wraps around to the next column in a Newspaper column format.

Figure 8.7

Hard Column code in a newspaper column format.

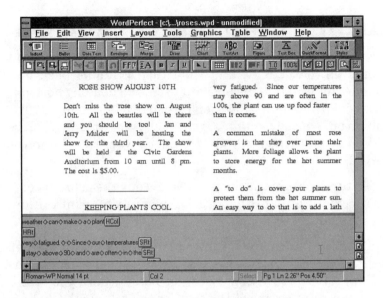

If you are using Balanced Newspaper format, you'll quickly find that the columns balance themselves. As you type, text spreads evenly between the columns. When you want to start over at the first column (probably at the end of the page), just press Ctrl+⏎Enter for hard column breaks until you're back at the first column.

TIP: Be careful when editing column text. Don't remove the important codes by accident.

Tables

An attractive way to organize information is to use the *Tables* feature. Rather than having you lay out information using tabs or parallel columns, this feature creates a table grid for you. Text you enter wraps around from one column to the next, until you indicate you want to go to a new part of the grid. You can also enter formulas in tables for quick math calculations. Figure 8.8 shows a simple table. This table shows a small budget. The totals in the last line were calculated with formulas entered into the table.

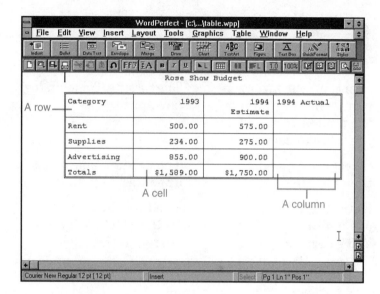

Figure 8.8
A simple table.

As shown in Figure 8.8, tables are organized into rows, columns, and cells. A *row* is a single line of boxes across the table. For example, Figure 8.8 shows a row for **Category**. A *column* refers to a vertical stack of boxes in the table. In the figure, the **1994 Actual** cells are in a column. A *cell* is a particular rectangular space in the table. In Figure 8.8, the total for the 1993 column (**1,589.00**) is contained in one cell.

Creative Uses for Tables

In addition to budgets, you can use tables to create inventory lists, expense accounts, financial reports, telephone lists, class enrollments, or employee lists.

Creating a table in WordPerfect for Windows is very straight-forward; you just tell it how many rows and how many columns you want. To create a table, follow the next Quick Steps.

Creating a Table

1. Position your insertion point where you want the top left corner of the table to begin.

   The Create Table dialog box appears.

2. Select Table, and then Create.

   The Create Table dialog box appears.

3. Enter the number of Columns and Rows, and select OK.

   The table appears. **Tbl Del:** and **Tbl Off** codes surround the table.

Once the grid is created, you can use regular WordPerfect for Windows features to enter information.

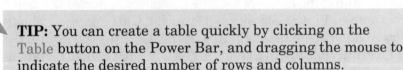

TIP: You can create a table quickly by clicking on the Table button on the Power Bar, and dragging the mouse to indicate the desired number of rows and columns.

Enter a Formula

To add a formula, you need to understand how each cell is identified. Starting in the upper left corner, columns are represented by letters starting with A, and rows are represented by numbers starting with 1. The cell in the upper left corner of the screen is A1, the next cell to the right is B1. The cell below A1 is A2 and so on. These are the *cell addresses*. See Figure 8.9.

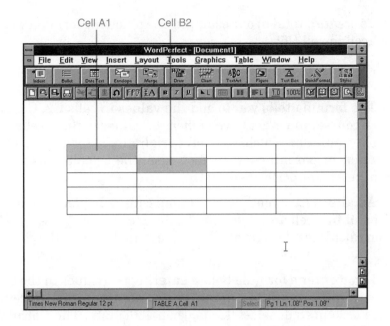

Figure 8.9
Identifying cells.

You can enter text (numbers and letters) into the table just as you type regular WordPerfect text. To enter formulas, you must leave the document editing mode (by placing your insertion point in the cell for the formula, and either pressing Ctrl + F12 or selecting Table, then Cell Formula Entry). When you are in Cell Formula Entry mode, that option is checked on the Table menu. You can enter a simple formula involving cell addresses and common math symbols. As you enter the formula, it appears in the cell. When you move the insertion point from the cell, the result of the formula appears. When you move the insertion point back into the cell, the formula appears in the status line.

You can use these symbols in formulas:

+	Add
–	Subtract (or negative number)
*	Multiply
/	Divide

To create a total in our example, the following formula would be placed in cell C5:

C2+C3+C4

The formula tells you to add the values in cells C2, C3, and C4. (Of course, you must have *numerical* values in these cells, not text.) Formulas are calculated left to right, unless you put part of a formula in parentheses. In that case, the calculations in the parentheses are performed first.

An alternative method for adding cells is to place the insertion point in a cell and select Table, Sum (or press Ctrl+=). The option calculates the sum of cells above or to the left of the current cell.

If you enter a formula before entering the values in the cells involved in the formula, you must calculate the result. Once the values are entered, select Table, then Calculate. The Calculate dialog box appears. Select Calc Table or Calc Document to calculate the existing formulas. If you want to calculate the table or document automatically in the future, select the appropriate Automatic Calculation Mode. Select OK.

You may also copy a formula. Place the insertion point in the cell with the formula you want to copy. Select Table, then Copy Formula. On the Copy Formula dialog box, identify a cell destinations. Select OK.

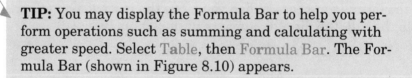

TIP: You may display the Formula Bar to help you perform operations such as summing and calculating with greater speed. Select Table, then Formula Bar. The Formula Bar (shown in Figure 8.10) appears.

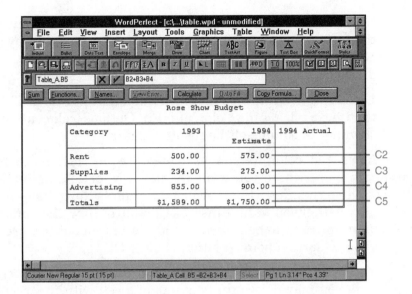

Figure 8.10
Identifying cells.

Editing a Table

Use the normal WordPerfect editing tools for entering and editing table text, as well as formatting. You can control the formatting of a single cell, or a number of cells you select (for example, an entire row or column). *Formatting* includes appearance, size, justification, adding columns, and so on.

From the **T**able menu, these editing options are available. When each is selected, you will first identify the cell(s) to affect (such as **C**ell, Co**l**umn, **R**ow, or the entire **T**able). Alternatively, you may select cells to affect before making the **T**able menu selection. From the **T**able menu, these editing options are available:

- **Format:** From the Format dialog box, identify the Alignment of cell contents. Select those Appearance options desired (such as Bold) and the Text Size. Indicate whether to Lock the cell(s) so they can't be changed. Identify whether to Ignore Cell When Calculating (such as a title cell containing numbers).

- **Nu**mber Type: From the Number Type dialog box, identify the type of numbering (such as **Cu**rrency, which displays 1200 as **$1,200**). The number type is previewed on the dialog box.

- **L**ines/Fill: From the Table Lines/Fill dialog box, identify the Line Styles, Line Color, and Fill Options (cell content shading). A sample of the result appears.

Rows and columns can be added. To do this, place the insertion point where you want the new row or column added. Select Table, then Insert. On the Insert Columns/Rows dialog box, identify whether you want to insert a **C**olumn or **R**ow, the number of columns or rows to be inserted, and the Placement (**B**efore or **A**fter your insertion point position). Select OK.

You may delete rows, columns, or the contents of cells. Although you may delete the contents of a cell with the Del or ◆Backspace key, the formula or formatting may hang on. Use the **D**elete command to delete all cell contents. To delete, select **D**elete from the Table menu. On the Delete dialog box, identify whether you want to delete Columns or Rows, and the number of columns or rows. The other alternative is to identify that you want to delete Cell Contents. Select OK.

Finally, you may use the Table menu to join or split tables: select **J**oin or **S**plit from the menu.

Table Shortcuts

When you begin to use very large tables, you'll want to speed up your work. Table 8.1 lists several of the quick movement keys.

Press	To move insertion point
Alt+arrow	To move to a cell up, down, left, or right.
Home, Home	To move to the first cell in a row.
End, End	To move to the last cell in a row.
Alt, Home	To move to the top line of a multi-line cell.
Alt, End	To move to the last line in multi-line cell.

Table 8.1
Quick Movement in a Table

Creating a Page Break

- Press Ctrl+↵Enter.

Go to a Page

1. Press Ctrl+G, or select Go to from the Edit menu.
2. Type the Page Number you want, and press ↵Enter.

Keeping Text Together

1. Position your insertion point (select text for Block Protect).
2. Select Layout, Page, and Keep Together Text.
3. Check the option for Widow/Orphan protection, Block Protect, or Conditional End of Page, and select OK.

Suppressing a Page Number on a Single Page

1. Select Layout, Page, Suppress.
2. Select Page Numbering, and complete the options.

Forcing an Odd or Even Page

1. Select Layout, Page, Force Page.
2. Select Current Page Odd or Current Page Even.

Working with Multiple-Page Documents

As you become skilled with WordPerfect for Windows, you will use it for pages and pages of work. In this chapter, you will learn not only how to create multiple pages, but also how to control the amount of text on the pages, go to a specific page, and print a group of pages. You'll also learn all about page numbering in WordPerfect for Windows.

Creating Multiple Pages

So far, you've learned to create and print a document, complete with the tab settings of your choice. Now you're ready to create a document that is more than one page long.

WordPerfect for Windows allows you to create lengthy documents; the maximum length depends only upon your computer's storage and memory capacity. Usually, though, any document over fifty pages seems a bit cumbersome; it takes too long to move around the document, and to make the frequent saves necessary to protect it.

In a long document, the pages appear on-screen one after another. Think of your document as a long scroll, with lines marking the pages.

> ### Using Different Page Formats in One Document
>
> The pages in a document do not necessarily have to be printed on the same type of paper, nor do they need to have the same formatting. For example, one document may have a letter to be printed on letterhead on the first page. The margins would be set up to fit the letter on the letterhead. The second page of the document may contain the address for an envelope, and include selected options appropriate to the envelope—a code for a different size or type of paper, different margins, and a copy of the letter's address to be printed on the envelope. The last page of the document may be a multiple-page report for regular 8.5-by-11-inch paper. A new code for paper size and type would be used, along with different margins, and page-numbering specific to the report.

There is more than one way to break a page. If you've been experimenting on your own, you may have already created an extra page by using WordPerfect's *automatic page break* feature.

Automatic Page Breaks

WordPerfect knows how many lines of text can fit on a page. The total is a careful calculation of the paper size minus the margins; both are set through the **Layout** menu, and covered in earlier chapters. The **Ln** amount in the lower right corner of the screen shows how many inches of the page (up to your insertion point position) have been filled with text.

On a typical 11-inch piece of paper with 1-inch margins at the top and bottom, you will be able to type to about the 9-inch mark before WordPerfect inserts an automatic page break. The exact measure varies according to the line spacing you're using (such as single or double), and the line height. Both are set through the

Layout menu, **L**ine command. If you edit the page and add or delete lines of text, the page break remains at the same line. The text, in effect, moves to fill the page.

On your screen in Page mode, an automatic page break appears as a line, as shown in Figure 9.1. (In Draft mode, the page break is a single line.) Notice that on the Reveal Codes screen, the automatic page break is shown as **HRt-SPg** (for a soft page break). *Soft page break* is WordPerfect jargon for a page break inserted automatically. If you insert a page break manually, this is referred to as a *hard page break*.

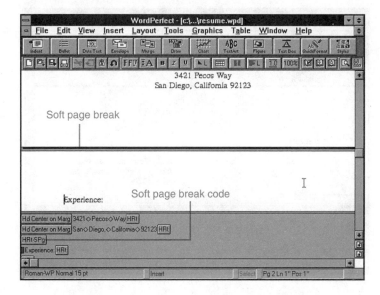

Figure 9.1
Automatic page break.

Manual Page Breaks

Often you will want a page break before WordPerfect enters one. For example, when you create a letter with several attachments, you may want to put the letter on the first page of the document and the attachments on subsequent pages, keeping all the related material in one WordPerfect document. When you print, you can insert letterhead for the first page and plain sheets after that.

Of course, you can press ⏎Enter enough times to take advantage of WordPerfect's automatic page break, but editing the text later could throw off the pages. Instead, use a manual (hard) page break.

To break a page manually, place the insertion point on the line and column where you want the page to be broken. Press Ctrl+⏎Enter. A double line (as shown in Figure 9.2) is inserted, and the **HPg** (hard page break) code is inserted into your document. Alternatively, select Layout, Page, Force Page, then New Page. The **Force: New** code is placed in the document, along with a double line. Whichever method you use, text appears after the manual page break, starting with the character your insertion point is on. If you want to get rid of the manual page break, just delete the code.

Figure 9.2

*Manual (hard)
page break.*

Hard page break

Hard page break code

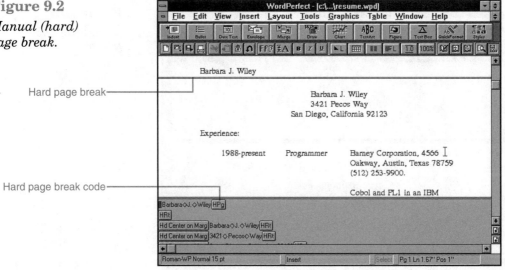

You may want a blank page in your document as a separator, or as a place to paste up an exhibit later. To create a blank page, just enter two hard page breaks. For more blank pages, enter as many hard page breaks as you need. If you are using blank pages (or pages with a good deal of "white space"), you may want to work in **D**raft mode, set through the **V**iew menu. If you use **D**raft mode, you will be able to see more of your document on the screen at one time than you do when working in **P**age mode.

Moving Between Pages

Once you have multiple pages, you will want to be able to move from page to page quickly. The number of the page appears in the bottom right corner of your screen. In this sample line:

Pg 4 Ln 8" Pos 3"

your insertion point is shown to be on page 4. To go directly to page 15, press Ctrl+G, or select Go To from the Edit menu. The Go To dialog box appears; you can enter the page to which you want to go. Select Page Number, type 15, and press ↵Enter. Your insertion point goes to the upper left corner of the first line of page 15 (unless you select another Position on the Go To dialog box). Now the line reads:

Pg 15 Ln 1" Pos 1"

Preventing Widows and Orphans

To many beginning users, the terms *widows* and *orphans* have to do only with women who have lost their mates and children who have lost their parents. In word processing, the terms also have to do with losses: specifically, when a single line of a paragraph has been lost to (split off from) the rest of its paragraph by a page break. A widow is the first line of a paragraph alone at the end of a page. An orphan is the last line of a paragraph isolated at the top of a page.

If you don't like the appearance of these textual widows and orphans, you can ask WordPerfect to prevent them. The following Quick Steps detail how to protect against widows and orphans.

QUICK STEPS   **Enabling Widow/Orphan Protection**

1. Put the insertion point where you want protection to start. Choose Layout, Page, Keep Text Together.

   The Keep Text Together dialog box appears.

2. Place a check in the Widow/Orphan Protect check box; select OK to return to your document.

   A **Wid/Orph: On** code is inserted into your text. To turn protection off, deselect the check box.

TIP: To protect an entire document, place the widow/orphan code at the beginning of the document.

Conditional End of Page

Sometimes you will want to keep several lines together in a document, even if it means letting a page run a little short. For example, in Figure 9.3, part of the sample résumé is split by a soft page break that WordPerfect inserted automatically. The split is inappropriate. To keep the lines together, you could insert a manual page break above the lines. The problem with this approach is that if you edit text, the hard page break may end up cutting the page too short. A better solution is to enter a *conditional end of page*, which keeps together the number of lines you specify, so that they can't be split between pages.

The following Quick Steps detail how to enter a conditional end of page. For our example, we'll keep the lines at the bottom of Figure 9.3 together.

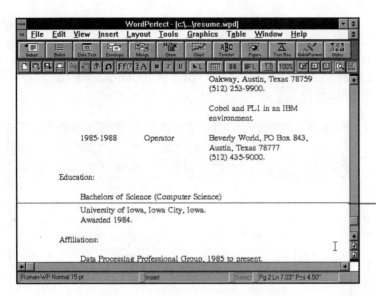

Figure 9.3

Résumé lines split by soft page break.

Soft page break

Entering a Conditional End of Page

1. Identify the number of lines to keep together, and place the insertion point before the first line.

The lines after the insertion point will be affected.

2. Choose Layout, Page, Keep Text Together.

The Keep Text Together dialog box appears.

3. Check the Conditional End of Page check box, enter the number of lines to be kept together, and choose OK.

The lines to keep together are identified.

4. Select OK to return to your document.

You are returned to your document, and the lines are kept together.

Figure 9.4 shows the résumé after the conditional end of page code has been inserted. Notice the code placement. The code **Condl EOP:5** appears, indicating that five lines are to be kept together. The text that was split is moved past the page break automatically.

Figure 9.4

Résumé lines after inserting conditional end of page.

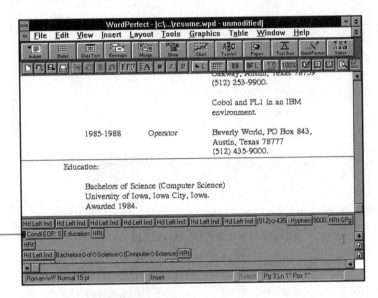

Conditional end of page code

Block Protection

You may want to keep a given block of text together (versus specifying a particular number of lines). If so, use the *block protect* feature instead of the conditional end of page feature. With block protect, you can change the number of lines in the block through editing, and the block will remain together on a single page.

This feature is especially useful for tables, or for any block that can be edited to a different number of lines. For example, Figure 9.5 shows text in a block protect. The entire block was moved to the start of a page. Notice the **BlockPro** codes that mark the beginning and end of the block.

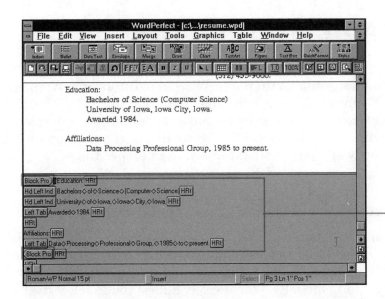

Figure 9.5
Block-protected text.

Block protection codes

TIP: Since the text you are block-protecting is to be placed on one page, you cannot apply block protection to more than a pageful of text.

The following Quick Steps detail how to block-protect text.

Using Block Protection

1. Select the text with [F8] or the mouse.

   The selected text is highlighted.

2. Select Layout, Page, and Keep Text Together.

   The Keep Text Together dialog box appears.

3. Check the Block Protect check box, and then select OK to return to your document.

   The block protection codes are inserted.

Page Numbering

Once you develop documents with multiple pages, you will want to be able to number the pages. With just a little setup, WordPerfect for Windows does this for you automatically. You'll be able to select from a variety of page number appearances, or develop your own unique look. In addition, you can insert a page number into the body of a page automatically, to reference the page.

Page Number Choices

Numbering pages is handy for short documents, and essential for most long documents. But don't number each page in the document tediously by hand. Instead, have WordPerfect number your pages automatically. WordPerfect allows you to select the following:

- Position of the number on the page.

- Options for the type of number—Roman, numbers, and letter—and a choice of formats (number alone or accompanied by text).

- The value of the number with which to start consecutive numbering.

You can change these options on any page you like, and as often as you like in a document. A new code is inserted each time you enter page-numbering options. The code affects the page on which it is entered, and all following text until a new code is encountered.

CAUTION   Place the codes controlling page numbering at the top of a page. If you put text before the page codes (or use conflicting page-numbering codes by accident), the page numbers may not print as you anticipated.

Adding a Page Number

> **Tip:** Page numbers do not appear in **D**raft mode. They only appear in **P**age mode and **T**wo Page mode. Change the mode by selecting **V**iew, and then the mode desired.

Let's start with a basic, no-frills page number. Here are the steps.

1. Place the insertion point before any existing text at the top of the page where you want page numbering to begin.

2. Select Layout, Page, and Numbering. The Page Numbering dialog box appears (see Figure 9.6).

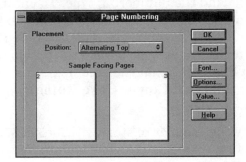

Figure 9.6

The Page Numbering dialog box.

3. Choose Position, then select the position of the page number (or no page number) in the drop-down list. The page number appears in the Sample Facing Pages on the Page Numbering dialog box. (Notice in Figure 9.6 that **Alternating Top** was selected as the **P**osition.)

4. To select the type of numbering (Roman, numbers, or letter), select Options. The Page Numbering Options dialog box (shown in Figure 9.7) appears.

Figure 9.7

*Page Numbering
Options dialog box.*

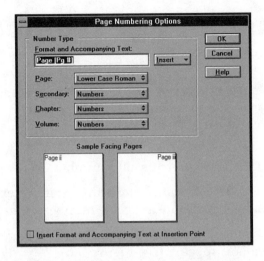

5. Select Page and the numbering type. To enter text before,
   after or around the page number, type the text in the
   Format and Accompanying Text text box. Select OK. The
   Sample Facing Pages appear with the options selected.
   (Notice in Figure 9.7 that the accompanying text **Page**
   was added, and that **Lower Case Roman** was selected as
   the Number Type.)

6. To identify the number to start with, select Value from the
   Page Numbering dialog box. The Numbering Value dialog
   box (shown in Figure 9.8) appears.

Figure 9.8

*Numbering Value
dialog box.*

7. Enter the value in New Page Number (or you may choose to Increase/Decrease Existing Page Number by a value). Select OK. You are returned to the Page Numbering dialog box.

8. Select OK to return to your document.

You may want to check Reveal Codes to ensure that all the selections are as you want. In the example shown in Figure 9.9, you can see codes placed in the document to yield an alternating page number, beginning with Roman numerals after the text (Page - iii), at the top of the page. The codes govern the page numbering until you enter new codes.

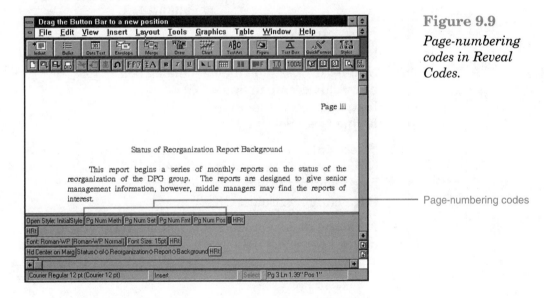

Figure 9.9

Page-numbering codes in Reveal Codes.

Page-numbering codes

The following Quick Steps summarize the page-numbering process. More details about some of the complex steps follow in later sections of this chapter.

Using Page Numbering

1. Place your insertion point at the top of a page.

2. Press Layout, Page, Numbering. | The Page Numbering dialog box appears.

3. Select a Position alternative. | The position of the page numbers appear in the Sample Facing Pages on the Page Numbering dialog box.

4. Choose the Options button to go to the Page Numbering Options dialog box. Add accompanying text, and select the numbering type. Select OK. | You are returned to the Page Numbering dialog box.

5. Select Value to go to the Numbering Value dialog box; identify the New Page Number. Select OK. | You are returned to the Page Numbering dialog box.

6. From the Page Numbering dialog box, select OK. | You are returned to your document.

Position on the Page

When it comes to positioning the page number, you are offered a variety of selections on the Page Numbering dialog box. They are:

No Page Number	Top Left	Top Center
Top Right	Alternating Top	Bottom Left
Bottom Center	Bottom Right	Alternating Bottom

If you are printing pages that will be copied double-sided, use the alternating page numbers. This way, the page number will appear on the upper outside (alternating top) of the page, or the lower outside (alternating bottom).

If you choose No Page Number, you can skip page numbers for one or more pages.

Numbering Type

When you select Options from the Page Numbering dialog box, you may use the Page Numbering Options dialog box to identify the type of numbering. The numbering type can be numbers (1, 2, 3), Roman numerals (I, II, III), or letters (A, B, C). Roman numerals and letters can be upper- or lowercase.

For example, you might have several WordPerfect documents making up one long, printed document. The first three pages of the first documents introduction are numbered **i**, **ii**, and **iii**, and the next 15 pages in the document can be numbered **1** through **15**. You then would want the first WordPerfect page of the second document to be numbered as page **16**, with consecutive numbering continuing from there.

Page Number Format and Accompanying Text

The Page Numbering Options dialog box may also be used to identify the page number format and accompanying text. This WordPerfect option allows you to enter the page number alone, or to enter text along with the page number. As an example, you may want the first three pages of a document to have this text along with the page number:

Appendix A—Page 1
Appendix A—Page 2
Appendix A—Page 3

On the fourth page, you may want to change to the following format and continue it through the rest of the document:

Appendix B—Page 1

The text ("Appendix") is just one way to use the page number format feature with text and symbols. (You can enter any text, up to approximately forty characters in length.) For instance, you may want to insert:

a date: June 10, 1993 (1)

a copyright notice: 1994 Alpha / Pg 1

the author's name: By Kate Miller p. #1

a confidential notification: CONFIDENTIAL: 1

identify the document as a draft: !!!! DRAFT !!!! p. 1

or just add a decoration to the page number: *** 1 ***

TIP: You may want to enter several lines of text along with a page number. If so, check out the discussion of headers and footers in Chapter 10.

When you set the format in WordPerfect, you enter the text before or after the existing symbol for the page number (that is **[Pg #]**). When you enter a new page number format, this type of code is placed in the document: **Pg Num Fmt**.

Numbering Value

The **V**alue button on the Page Numbering dialog box takes you to the Numbering Value dialog box. This is where you can select the page number you want to start with at a given point in the document. You may set a new page number, or simply choose to increase or decrease the existing page number by a value you enter.

Inserting New Pages After Pages Are Numbered

What if you create a lengthy document with consecutive page numbering, and want to insert pages later? If renumbering the document would take too long, or multiple copies of the existing document have been distributed, add pages in-between. For example, pages 17.1 through 17.5 could be added between page 17 and page 18.

You could type in page numbers for these pages. That would, however, leave some pages governed by automatic page number, and others with page numbers typed in. If you wanted to print the document later, considerable editing would have to be done first to standardize the way page numbers are assigned.

Instead, use WordPerfect's page-numbering options to add a new page number with the appropriate format. Continuing the example of adding pages 17.1 through 17.5, enter a code on what is to be page 17.1. Select a new Page Number of 1 (this will become the .1, .2, and so on). Enter a Page Number Format of 17.[Pg #]. After what is now page 17.5, enter a code with new Page Number set to 18 to return to the correct consecutive page numbering. When you print the pages they will be numbered correctly.

The specially-numbered page codes can be easily removed. In Chapter 12 you will learn how to search for codes. If you end up with a document with multiple page changes, and you want to remove inserted page numbering, just search out the page codes, and edit as you want.

Forcing an Odd or Even Page

You may want to force a page to be odd or even. For example, it is customary for first pages of double-sided chapters to be odd pages.

This way, the first page of each chapter starts on the right side of the open book. To force an odd or even page, put your insertion point on the page. Select Page, then Force Page, from the **Layout** menu. On the Force Page dialog box, select Current Page Odd or Current Page Even. Select OK. If necessary, WordPerfect for Windows inserts a page break.

Controlling Page Number Fonts and Attributes

Whatever fonts and attributes are set prior to a page code affects the appearance of the page number. You can control the font or attributes of the page numbers. Select Layout, Page, and Numbering. On the Page Numbering dialog box, select Font. The Page Numbering Font dialog box appears. Here you can change the font and appearance. This dialog box works the same as the Font dialog box. For more information about the options, consult Chapter 6, Giving Characters a New Look.

Inserting the Page Number in the Body of the Page

For reference purposes, you may want to insert the page number in the body of the text. These phrases illustrate two examples:

Return to this page **(3)** when you have completed the test.

Remember that the instructions are here on **page 4**.

Use WordPerfect's features for inserting page numbers (instead of typing in the page numbers). That way, if the number of pages changes due to editing, the number that prints will always be correct. You can enter the page number without the accompanying text or with the accompanying text.

To enter the page number without the accompanying text, follow the next Quick Steps.

Entering the Page Number Only

1. Place the insertion point in the body of the text where the page number is to appear.

2. Select Layout, Page, and Numbering.

   The Page Numbering dialog box appears.

3. Select Value.

   The Numbering Value dialog box appears.

4. Check Insert and Display at Insertion Point; select OK, then Close.

   You are returned to your document. The page number appears in your text in the formatting set for page numbering. The page number (without accompanying text, if any) appears between two codes like this:

   Pg Num Disp3Pg Num Disp

Entering the Page Number With Accompanying Text

1. Place the insertion point in the body of the text where the page number is to appear.

continues

continued

2. Select Layout, Page, and Numbering.	The Page Numbering dialog box appears.
3. Select Options.	The Page Numbering Options dialog box appears.
4. Check Insert Format and Accompanying Text at Insertion Point, and select OK twice.	You are returned to your document. The page number appears in your text with the accompanying text entered on the Options dialog box. The codes appear as: **Pg Num Disp**Page 3**Pg Num Disp Formatted Pg Num**

Suppressing Page Numbers

You may want to *suppress* a page number on one page. This is sometimes required if you want to place a large graphic on a page, or give the page a different look. When you suppress the page number on a page, that page number remains in the consecutive count. For example, if you suppress the page number on page 3, the pages will be numbered 1, 2, (page 3 will have no page number), 4, 5, and so on.

To suppress a page number, use the following Quick Steps.

QUICK STEPS

Suppressing a Page Number

1. Choose Layout, Page, Suppress.

   The Suppress dialog box appears.

2. Check Page Numbering and OK.

   The page number is suppressed, and the **Suppress: Page Num** code appears in your text.

Printing Multiple Pages

Printing multiple pages is simple. When you press F5 or select Print from the File menu, the Print dialog box appears. Choose Multiple Pages and complete the dialog box as usual. When you are ready to print, select the Print button. The Multiple Pages dialog box appears (see Figure 9.10).

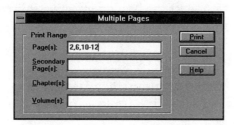

Figure 9.10

The Multiple Pages dialog box.

Enter the Print Range for Page(s). Place a dash between the first and last page in the range. Enter individual pages with commas separating each page number.

What Are Headers and Footers?

- A *header* is text that appears at the top of the document page (after the top margin).
- A *footer* appears at the bottom of the page (before the bottom margin).

Add a Header or Footer

1. Choose Layout then Header/Footer.
2. Select Header A, Header B, Footer A, or Footer B, then Create.
3. Enter the text, and enter values for Number, Placement, and Distance as appropriate.
4. Select Close when you are done.

Discontinue a Header or Footer

1. Select Layout, then Header/Footer.
2. Select the header or footer to discontinue, then select Discontinue.

Adding the Date

1. Select Insert, then Date.
2. Choose Date Text or Date Code.

Adding the Name of the File

1. Choose Other from the Insert menu.
2. Select Filename or Path and Filename.

The Professional Touch: Headers and Footers

If you create multiple-page documents such as reports or manuals, you will want to learn about the use of headers and footers. They add professionalism to any document. Better still, they aren't hard to master.

A *header* or *footer* is text that appears at the top (head) or the bottom (foot) of each page. Headers and footers can add a professional touch to a document, to give it a first-rate appearance. A header or footer can include the name of a document, version number, notification of status ("DRAFT" or "Confidential," for instance), author's name, page number, chapter or section numbers, graphics, or any other appropriate text you care to include. These are possible sample header or footer lines:

Chapter 3   page 316
CONFIDENTIAL from President's officepage 6 of 9
Year End Report   - DRAFT -   by Jim
Lindy

1993 Webber Corporation

A header or footer can be more than a single line; in fact, it can include up to one pageful of text. This allows you great flexibility in the amount of information you can place in a header or footer. When you create headers and footers, you can use all of WordPerfect's editing features.

When you place the header or footer in the document, a code appears in your document to mark the start of the header or footer. The header or footer is then repeated automatically, on each page or on alternating pages, depending on your selection. Every time you enter a new header or footer code, that header or footer is used until you enter another code.

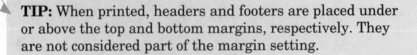

TIP: When printed, headers and footers are placed under or above the top and bottom margins, respectively. They are not considered part of the margin setting.

Creating a Header or Footer

Here's how to create a header or footer.

1. Place the insertion point at the top of the first page for the header or footer (before all codes except Paper Size/Type or Top/Bottom Margin codes).

2. From the Layout menu, select Header/Footer. The Headers/Footers dialog box appears.

3. Select whether you want to enter text for Header A, Header B, Footer A, or Footer B.

NOTE: You can place two headers or footers on a page—which is useful if you have entered one header as Header A, and then want to add more text to the header. Instead of editing it, you can add Header B. Get in the practice of always choosing Header A or Footer A first. Then, if a Header B or Footer B is necessary, you will know you are adding to the first header or footer on the page.

4. Select Create.

5. The header or footer window, complete with the Feature Bar, appears (see Figure 10.1). Enter the header or footer text, using any of WordPerfect's editing features.

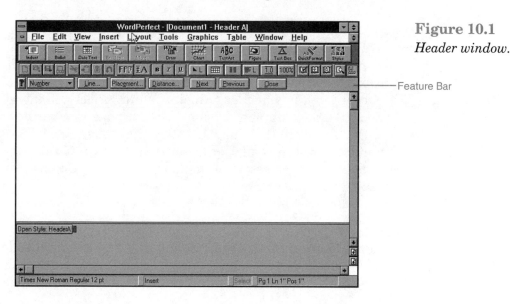

Figure 10.1
Header window.

6. To add a page number, place the insertion point where you want the number. Select Number, then Page Number.

7. Choose Placement on the Feature Bar. On the Placement dialog box, identify whether the header or footer should appear on Odd Pages, Even Pages, or Every Page.

8. If you want to change the space between the header or footer and the text in the body of your document, select Distance. Enter the distance and select OK.

9. Once the header or footer text is complete, choose Close on the Feature Bar. A code for the header or footer is inserted.

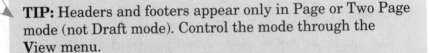

TIP: Headers and footers appear only in Page or Two Page mode (not Draft mode). Control the mode through the View menu.

TIP: To place a page number in the header or footer, select Number on the Feature Bar, and select Page Number. The code **Pg Num Disp 1** appears. Every time this symbol is encountered in a header or footer, WordPerfect will increment the page number by one. To start page numbering with a number other than 1, enter a new page number value before the header or footer code. The **Pg Num Set** code indicates the start of the new value. (See Chapter 9 to review this procedure.)

The following Quick Steps summarize how to add a header or footer.

Adding a Header or Footer

1. Place the insertion point in the location you want the header or footer to occupy on the page.

2. Select Header/Footer from the Layout menu.

   The Headers/Footers dialog box appears.

3. Select Header A, Header B, Footer A, or Footer B.

   The options for headers or footers become available.

4. Select Create.

   You are taken to the header or footer window.

5. Choose Number to add (insert) a Page Number. Choose Placement to select the pages for the header or footer. Choose Distance to change the space between the header or footer and the text.

   Options are set.

6. Enter the header or footer text, just as you would any WordPerfect text. When you are done, select Close to return to the document screen.

   A code for the header or footer is placed in your document.

Safety Checks for Headers and Footers

As you get accustomed to using headers and footers, you may find some surprising results when you print a document. For example, it is easy for a beginner to forget to consider the spacing between the header text and the body

continues

continued

of the document. It is also easy to forget that codes entered in the document after the header or footer code (such as those for margins or special fonts) will not take effect in the header or footer.

Follow these safety checks before you print. Check the Reveal Codes screen to make sure there are no unusual formatting codes placed accidentally around the header or footer. Make certain the header or footer code appears at the top of the page. Consider the formatting codes. Are the appropriate codes contained in the header or footer? Finally, check the appearance of the header or footer through View, Page or Two Page mode. Taking a few moments to double-check the setup of your header or footer can save paper and time.

Adding the Date

With WordPerfect for Windows, you can enter the current date automatically—as text (which doesn't change), or as a code (which reflects the current date). It is handy to use the date in a header or footer when a document will undergo several reviews; that way, the date of the current version is apparent. If you will print a document, the code is useful to indicate the print date.

To insert the date, place the insertion point in the location for the date. To insert the date as text, press Ctrl+D, or select Insert, Date, and Date Text. The text won't change over time. To insert the date as a code, press Ctrl+⇧Shift+D, or select Insert, Date, and Date Code. The code will ensure that the date will always reflect the current date.

To change the format (month, day, year), select Insert, Date, Date Format. Select the format you want, then choose OK.

Adding the Name of the File

When documents are printed and passed around, it is easy to lose track of the original file and its location. This is especially true in an organization using a large network. To avoid this problem, you can enter the filename or the path and filename in your document. A code is entered that reflects the current filename.

To enter the filename in your document, Choose Insert, Other. Then, choose Filename (for just the name) or Path and Filename (to include the path). The filename appears in the document, and a code is inserted. If you change the filename, the document is updated automatically.

Adding Graphic Effects

Although headers and footers are used typically to provide information, they can also be used for a pleasing graphic effect. You can use symbols created through WordPerfect's keyboard options (such as underlines or double underlines). Symbols from among the special characters supported by WordPerfect can be used. Or you can place sophisticated graphics (like those covered in Chapter 16, "Using Graphics in Your Document") in headers and footers. See Chapter 16 to learn how to use the Line option on the Feature Bar when in a header or footer window.

Though creating and inserting graphic effects can take some time, a well-designed header or footer can pay off in the professional look of a document, and in greater ease of use.

Editing Headers and Footers

Editing a header or footer is a lot like adding one. Follow these steps:

1. Place your insertion point after the code representing the header or footer you want to edit.

2. Select Layout, then Header/Footer.

3. Select whether you want to edit Header **A**, Header **B**, Footer A, or Footer B, and choose Edit.

4. Edit the header or footer window as you would any WordPerfect document screen. Change Number, Placement, and Distance as desired.

5. When you are done, select Close. The new, edited header or footer takes effect.

TIP: You may double-click on the code for a header or footer to edit it. You are immediately taken to the header or footer window.

Turning a Header or Footer Off

Discontinuing a header or footer is only slightly different from editing one. To turn a header or footer off:

1. Put your insertion point after the paragraph containing the header or footer code, at the location where you want to discontinue the header or footer. (You may also select pages.)

2. Select Header/Footer from the Layout menu.

3. Identify the header or footer to discontinue, then choose Discontinue. A code like this is placed in your text: **End Header A**.

You can also suppress a header or footer for a single page at a time. To do so:

1. Place the insertion point at the top of the page on which you want to suppress the header or footer.

2. Select Layout, Page, Suppress. The Suppress dialog box shown in Figure 10.2 appears.

3. Check the appropriate check boxes, and return to your document. A code is placed in the document.

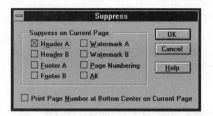

Figure 10.2
The Suppress dialog box.

Depending on the boxes you check, you can suppress (for example) a single header or footer, a combination of headers and footers, or all headers and footers on the page.

TIP: To delete a header or footer, just delete the code or drag it off the Reveal Codes window. But be careful to delete the correct one. If you delete the wrong one, use Undo or Undelete from the Edit menu. You can also copy and cut (move) header and footer codes. This is handy if you have developed a fancy header and want to use it in another document. Just copy it to the new document, and edit it for that document.

Checking Spelling

1. Select Speller from the Tools menu.
2. Select Check to identify the amount of text to check.
3. Select Start.

Checking the Spelling in Selected Text

1. Select the text with F8 or the mouse.
2. Choose Speller from the Tools menu.

Looking Up a Word

1. Choose Speller from the Tools menu.
2. Choose Check, Word, then Start.

Getting Document Information

1. Select Document Info from the File menu.

Checking Grammar

1. Choose Grammatik from the Tools menu.
2. Select Start.

Using the Thesaurus

1. Place your insertion point on the word to look up.
2. Select Thesaurus from the Tools menu.
3. Select an option.

Using the Writing Tools

Don't reach for that dictionary! Instead, use WordPerfect's *Spell Checker*. With it, you can check the spelling of a single word, a page, or an entire document. WordPerfect locates its built-in dictionary, looks up any unrecognized word, and suggests alternative spellings—more than any paper dictionary does. But that's not all; WordPerfect also comes with a handy thesaurus and a sophisticated grammar-checking program.

How Does the Spell Checker Work?

WordPerfect's spelling checker consists of a very long list of acceptable words. Every word in your document is checked against this list. If the word is found, WordPerfect goes on to the next word. If the word is not found, it notifies you, and you can skip the word, add it to the list, or make a correction.

In addition to checking spelling, WordPerfect finds double occurrences of a word, a common typographical error. In this next sentence, the word "the" was entered twice:

Politics is a risky business for the the faint of heart.

If you were to spell-check a document containing this sentence, WordPerfect would point out the redundant word, and enable you to fix the sentence.

Correcting Text

To begin the spell check, place your insertion point on the word, the page, or anywhere in the document. If you want to spell-check a selection of text, select it using F8 or the mouse.

TIP: Selecting text is useful when you've already spell-checked a document, edited a section, and now want to spell-check only that edited section.

Select Tools, then Speller. The Speller dialog box appears (see Figure 11.1).

Figure 11.1
The Speller dialog box after finding a misspelled word.

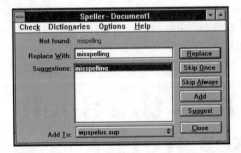

To identify what to spell-check, select Check. Select one of the following options.

Word: Checks the word where the insertion point rests.

Sentence: Checks the sentence in which the insertion point lies.

Paragraph: Checks the paragraph with your insertion point.

Page: Checks the page on which your insertion point rests.

Document: Checks the entire document.

To End of Document: Checks from the insertion point location to the end of the document.

Number of Pages: Allows you to enter a page range to check.

Once you have identified what to spell-check, select the Start command button on the Speller dialog box. The spell check begins. WordPerfect for Windows skips those words that match words in the dictionary. When WordPerfect hits a word that is not in its dictionary, the Speller dialog box (shown in Figure 11.1) appears. The word identified as misspelled ("mispelling" in this example) is highlighted.

This dialog box suggests spelling alternatives, and prompts you for the possible actions to take. You can select a suggested word and press ⏎Enter (or choose Replace). The word is replaced with the word suggested. Or, you may select from the following actions.

Skip Once: Skips this first occurrence of this word which is not identified in the dictionary.

Skip Always: Adds the word to a Document Specific dictionary so the word will be skipped when this document is checked.

Add: Adds the word to the current dictionary shown after Add To option. If you choose the supplementary dictionary, the word will be skipped in this and any other document you spell-check.

Suggest: Suggests other possible spelling alternatives. If there are more suggestions than can appear in the list, a scroll bar becomes available; use it to browse the list.

TIP: Adding your own name to the supplementary dictionary is a good use of the **Add** feature.

Replace With: If you don't like the alternatives WordPerfect presents, you can type in a word to use for the replacement. Don't worry about knowing how to spell what you're typing in, because suggestions will appear immediately in response to your entry. If you want to change more than just a word, you can click on the document and make corrections. Then click on the Resume button in the Speller dialog box to continue spell-checking from the position the check left off.

TIP: You can enter a word pattern instead of a word in the Replace With text box. This takes advantage of WordPerfect's ability to look up on phonetic matches. When you want to use a word pattern, use an asterisk (*) to stand for multiple characters, or a question mark (?) to stand for a single character. For example, looking up *ure will find words such as acupuncture, and adjure. Entering ?ure then pressing ⏎Enter finds word with a single letter followed by "ure," such as cure, lure, and pure. (Before you press ⏎Enter, WordPerfect doesn't know you are limiting the length of the word. Therefore, words like aureate, bureau, and bureaucracies appear.)

A common typing mistake is entering double words. If WordPerfect for Windows encounters a double word, choose one of these options from the Speller dialog box:

Skip One: To keep the duplication and continue with the spell check.

Replace: To delete the second occurrence of the word.

When it comes to capitalization, WordPerfect identifies both *capitalization differences* (words that are capitalized inconsistently) and *irregular case*—words that have odd capitalization (such as the appearance of the word SinCerely). For either problem, you may choose from the same options as during regular spell-checking.

TIP: If you want to quit the spell checker before it's finished, just press Close.

The Quick Steps that follow summarize the procedures for spell-checking, identifying words not in the WordPerfect for Windows dictionary, and responding to the words identified.

Spell Checking

1. If you want, select the text with F8 or the mouse.

You have identified a selection of text to be spell-checked.

2. Choose Tools, then Speller.

The Speller dialog box appears. Otherwise, if you selected text, spell-checking begins (go on to step 4.)

3. If you did not select text, choose Check to identify the amount of text to check, then choose Start.

The first unrecognized word is found.

4. Replace the word or make another selection.

Your selection is carried out. Spell-checking continues until the final word is checked, and you are informed that the spell check is complete.

5. Select Yes to close the Speller.

TIP: You may customize how the spell checker behaves. From the Speller dialog box, select Options. Check the options you want handled by the speller. These include spell-checking words with numbers, and beeping to signal misspellings.

Creating Supplementary Dictionaries

Using *supplementary dictionaries* opens a whole area of power you might not expect. You can add or change words in supplementary dictionaries. You can also add words to replace others automatically, or to supply as alternatives. For example, you may want to type the acronym **HMO**, but have it appear on-screen as **Health Maintenance Organization**. You may also want WordPerfect to suggest alternatives to all occurrences of "i.e." An alternative might be "that is:".

When you add a word to the dictionary during spell-checking, it is saved in a file named WPSPELUS.SUP. As you add words, you are creating a personal supplementary dictionary.

To edit the supplementary dictionary (or create or edit another supplementary dictionary), select Speller from the Tools menu. On the Speller dialog box, select Dictionaries. Select Supplementary. The Supplementary Dictionaries dialog box appears. Select the dictionary you want (such as WPSPELUS.SUP), and choose Edit. The Edit - wpspelus.sup dialog box (shown in Figure 11.2) appears. This dialog box shows the words already in the supplementary dictionary you have chosen.

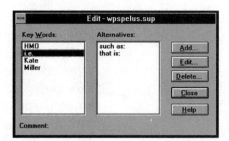

Figure 11.2
*The Edit -
wpspelus.sup dialog
box.*

For example, in Figure 11.2, **i.e.** has been entered as a Key **W**ord. When selected (as it is in the figure), the spell checker will suggest the Alternatives which have been entered (also shown).

To add new words to the supplementary dictionary, select Add. The Add Word/Phrase - wpspelus.sup dialog box appears (see Figure 11.3).

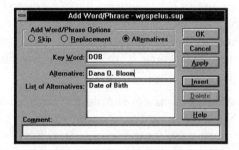

Figure 11.3
*The Add Word -
wpspelus.sup
dialog box.*

You choose to add any one of three types of words:

Skip: Words or phrases to skip during spell-checking.

Replacement: Words or phrases to be replaced during spell-checking, with the replacement identified through this dialog box.

Alternatives: Words or phrases to have alternates identified during spell-checking. The alternatives are identified through this dialog box. For example, type in a Key Word (in the example, it is DOB). Type in an Alternative and choose Insert. Continue typing in alternatives and choosing Insert until all are entered. Then choose Apply to add the information on alternatives to the supplementary dictionary.

If you want to edit the information in the supplementary dictionary later, use the Edit - wpspelus.sup dialog box. Highlight an existing word, and select Edit to edit the word (you can do the same with replacement or alternate words). To delete a word from the supplementary dictionary, highlight it on the same dialog box, and select Delete.

You may create another supplementary dictionary to be selected on the Speller dialog box. For example, you may want one supplementary dictionary for work with one client, and a different dictionary for another client. To create a dictionary, select Tools, then Speller. On the Speller dialog box, select Dictionaries, then Supplementary. On the Supplementary Dictionaries dialog box, select Create. You are taken to the Select/Create Supplementary Dictionary dialog box. From there, type in the new dictionary name in Filename (use the SUP file extension), select OK, and follow the prompts.

Looking Up a Word

You can look up a word as you work, rather than performing a full-blown spell check. To look up text you've entered, put the insertion point on the word. Select Speller from the Tools menu. Pick Check, then Word, then choose Start. A faster method is to select the word or phrase, then select Speller from the Tools menu. The word is immediately checked. You may also go to the Speller dialog box, and type in a new word or word pattern in the Replace With text box to see alternate spellings for the word you enter. As mentioned earlier, when you enter a word pattern, use an asterisk (*) to stand for multiple characters or a question mark (?) to stand for a single character.

Getting Document Information

WordPerfect supplies a good deal of information about your document. From the document, select Document Info from the File menu. The Document Information dialog box (shown in Figure 11.4) appears.

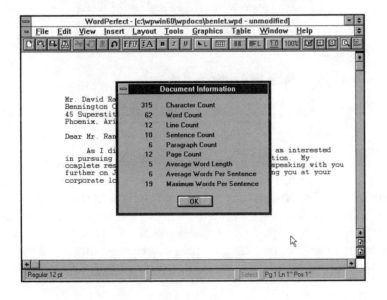

Figure 11.4

Information available through Document Information.

Checking Grammar

WordPerfect comes with the Grammatik grammar checker. It will identify sentences that are too lengthy, incorrect tense, omitted words, and other grammar concerns. For example, suppose we use Grammatik to check the grammar on this sentence:

I never seen him be long to a group before.

As shown in Figure 11.5, Grammatik stops at the word *seen*, and points out that the sentence doesn't have a main verb. The replacement *saw* is suggested.

Although Grammatik is smart—with hundreds of rules built in—it is not your eighth-grade language teacher. In our sentence example, Grammatik cannot identify that *be long* is really supposed to be the word *belong*. When you use Grammatik, remember that it is giving you suggestions. Use your own judgment in correcting text.

Figure 11.5

The Grammatik dialog box, and portion of the document being checked.

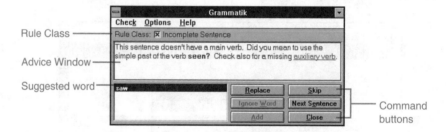

The document window is shown with the Grammatik dialog box in Figure 11.5. The portion of your document being checked is highlighted. The *Rule Class* indicates the class of the grammatical rule being applied—in this case, the rules for Incomplete Sentence. The *Advice Window* provides commentary on the identified grammar problem. In this example, there is a suggested replacement. The *command buttons* show your options for continuing.

The following Quick Steps summarize the procedure for checking grammar.

Checking Grammar

1. With your insertion point in the document, select Tools, then Grammatik.

   The Grammatik dialog box appears.

2. Select Start.

   Grammatik begins checking the document.

3. The first possible grammar problem is identified. Advice is given, and suggestions may be available. Use the options at the bottom of the screen to make a change, or continue to the next problem.

   You are notified when grammar checking is completed and you may close Grammatik.

4. Select Yes to close Grammatik.

   You are returned to your WordPerfect for Windows document. Any changes you made are placed in the document.

Thesaurus

WordPerfect's *Thesaurus* feature is simple to use and often overlooked. When you say, "That's not quite the word I want," call up WordPerfect's Thesaurus for other suggestions.

The following Quick Steps detail how to use the Thesaurus.

Using the Thesaurus

1. Place your insertion point on the word you want to look up, and select Thesaurus from the Tools menu.	Suggested replacements for the word appear.
2. Select one of the options shown at the bottom of the screen.	Prompts for the selected operation appear. Follow the prompts to complete the operation.

The following is a list of the available buttons from within Thesaurus:

Replace: This button replaces the word in your document with the one highlighted.

Look Up: In the Word text box, type in a different word (or select a word shown in the lists) and select Look Up. Suggested substitutions for that new word appear.

Close: This button lets you stop using the Thesaurus and return to your document without substituting a word.

To see a list of words that have been looked up, select the History menu. Then, to go to the list of words, select any word that appears.

If you fill more than the three columns with suggested words, you can press the ← or → keys to move from column to column. Or use the mouse, and click on the left or right arrow.

Finding

1. Select text within which to search (if desired) with F8 or the mouse.
2. Press F2, or select Find from the Edit menu.
3. Enter the text to Find. (Use Type or Match to narrow the find or add codes. Use Options to identify what text to find.)
4. Select Find Next or Find Prev to search forward or backward.

Replacing

1. Select text, if desired, with F8 or the mouse.
2. Press Ctrl+F2, or select Replace from the Edit menu.
3. Enter the text to Find and Replace With. (Use Type or Match to narrow the find or add codes. Use Options to identify what text to find. Use Direction to identify the direction of the search.)
4. Select Find to find the first occurrence, or Replace All to replace all occurrences.

Entering Bookmarks

- To enter a QuickMark, press Ctrl+⇧Shift+Q.
- To create and enter a bookmark, select Bookmark from the Insert menu. Select Create and enter a bookmark name.

Finding and Replacing

Finding and replacing characters is a feature that, at first, you may not think you'll use often. Read on. In this chapter, you will learn not only how to use Find and Replace, but you will also gain ideas about how to use Find and Replace creatively to solve problems.

You use WordPerfect for Windows' *Find* feature to find text and codes in a document. You type in the text or codes you want to find, and WordPerfect locates the first occurrence. If you want, you can then continue searching from that location.

There are more uses for Find than may meet the eye. You can find text that you believe may be incorrectly entered. Or you can find a key word in order to move to a particular spot in a document. Find is also useful for checking headings, figure numbering, or bulleted text against tables of contents or indexes.

Using Find to Search for Special Spots

You may need to go from one part of a lengthy document to another to check information, and then return to your original spot. If so, you can place a Bookmark, QuickMark, or Comment in your text (each is described later in this chapter). For a quick notation, however, just enter special text in that special spot.

Here's how to proceed. Place the special text at the point to which you want to return. Make sure the characters are unique, and won't be used elsewhere in the document. Some users like to use a double asterisk and their name or instructions as a bookmark (such as ****Bill:check this out**). Go wherever you want in your document. Then, when you want to go back to the special spot, simply find the unique characters. Remember, you are just finding a series of characters. (The down side of this approach is that you must remember to delete all the special text before you are done with the document. Otherwise, the special text will appear in the document when printed.)

Figure 12.1 illustrates one use of Find. Here, the document will be checked for "Bennington" being misspelled as "Benningtin." Notice that the Find: text box shows the text that is sought. The message in Figure 12.2 shows that the spelling is not found. You know that in this document, at least, "Bennington" is not "Benningtin."

The *Replace* feature goes a step beyond searching. With it, you identify both the text you want to find, and the text that is to replace the found text. Replace is useful if you realize a proper name is misspelled consistently, a code is incorrectly used, or you want to change formatting. For example, for a bulleted list, you might have entered text with a small o (for the bullet) followed by a tab. In order to change that to a dash followed by an indent, you could use Replace.

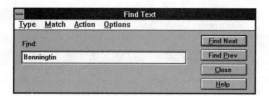

Figure 12.1
Using the Find Text dialog box to check for "Benningtin."

Figure 12.2
"Benningtin" was not found.

Let's take a look at an example. In our letter, bullets are created by a dash followed by an indent. We'll replace those with a small *o* and an indent. Figure 12.3 shows the text that will be found, and the replacement we'll use. We include the indent after the dash because we want to find only those occurrences where the dash is followed by an indent (not dashes that might be hyphens, for example). Figure 12.4 illustrates the text after the replacement is made. Notice that the small *o*s are now included.

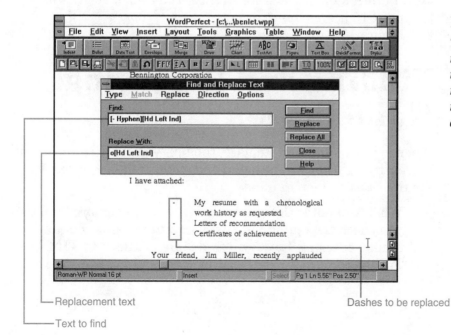

Figure 12.3
The dash and indent entered for the search, to be replaced by an indent, small o, and indent.

Replacement text

Text to find

Dashes to be replaced

Figure 12.4
After replacements.

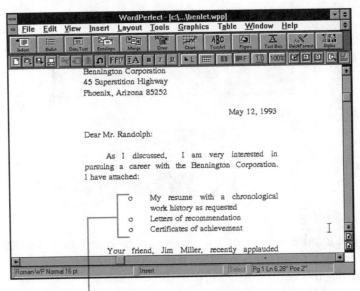

The dashes have been changed to bullets.

You can check your replacements as you work, or let WordPerfect for Windows do it alone. If you check replacements, WordPerfect stops at each occurrence. You then identify whether to replace that occurrence or not.

Finding and Replacing Guidelines

When you use Find and Replace, the text you enter is important to identifying what will be found and, potentially, replaced. Here are the rules to keep in mind:

- When you enter the text to find, the case is ignored unless you check the option for a *case-sensitive* search. For example, entering Time will find **time**, **Time**, and **TIME**. For the find to be case-sensitive, you will need to select

Match, Case. Then the find will yield an exact match to your entry.

- Found text will locate *portions* of larger words. Select Match, Whole Word to locate only complete words (not parts of words). For example, entering like will find **alike**, **businesslike**, and **dislike**. Selecting for whole words will find only **like**.

- When text is replaced, the *case* used in the replacement will match the replaced text. (For example, if **Merger** is encountered, and you are replacing with the word "consolidation," the replacement is entered with the first letter capitalized, as in the text being replaced.)

- Pay attention to your use of *spaces* when you use Find. If you enter spaces, the spaces will be included in the search. If you leave out spaces, words that include the specified text will be found.

- To match on *codes* (including font codes), you will need to select the appropriate codes from the options available. Use Match, Font to find font codes. Use Match, Codes to find most codes. Or use Type, Specific Codes to limit code selection to the specific values you enter (such as a bottom margin of 1.5 inches).

- Identify what text to search with Options. The alternatives are:

  Begin Find at Top of Document: Starts at the top of the document instead at the insertion point location.

  Wrap at Beg./End of Document: After reaching the end of the document, the search continues at the top.

  Limit Find Within Selection: Once text is selected, only the selected text is found.

  Include Headers, Footers, etc. in Find: Includes the headers and footers in the search.

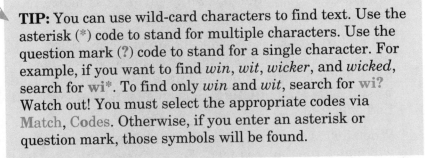

TIP: You can use wild-card characters to find text. Use the asterisk (*) code to stand for multiple characters. Use the question mark (?) code to stand for a single character. For example, if you want to find *win*, *wit*, *wicker*, and *wicked*, search for **wi***. To find only *win* and *wit*, search for **wi?** Watch out! You must select the appropriate codes via Match, Codes. Otherwise, if you enter an asterisk or question mark, those symbols will be found.

Finding Text

On a Find, you'll use Find Next to search forward or Find Prev to search backward. The following Quick Steps summarize how to find text in a document.

---

*Q*UICK STEPS   **Using Find**

1. Select text to search, if desired. Press F2, or select Find from the Edit menu.

   The Find Text dialog box appears.

2. Enter the text and codes you want to Find. (Use Match to control Whole Words, Case, or to find a Font or Code. Use Type, Specific Codes to specify codes with values. Use Options to choose the extent of the search.)

   The text and/or codes to be found and the extent of the search is identified.

3. Select Find Next to search forward, or Find Prev to search backward.

   The text is found.

Using Find to Select Text

You can select text the old fashioned way . . . or with Find. Suppose you know the last word or phrase you want to include in the selected text. Position the insertion point at the beginning of the selection. Press F2 for the Find Text dialog box. Enter the last word or phrase in the selection, and choose Action, Extend Selection. Select Find Next. The selection is extended to the text identified. Make sure to select Action, Select Match when you want to find text in the future (rather than extending a selection from your insertion point).

Finding Codes

As mentioned earlier, you can enter codes you want found or replaced. It can be a little confusing, however, deciding whether to use Match, Codes or Type, Specific Codes. Both options are available on the Find Text and the Find and Replace Text dialog boxes.

The Match, Codes selection displays the Codes dialog box. You may scroll through the list to find the code you want, or (to go directly to the choice) just begin typing in the code. Once the code you want to find is located, select Insert. The code is placed in the Find text box. The codes available through Match, Codes include * (the wildcard for many characters), ? (the wildcard for a single character), and codes that can be found in WordPerfect for Windows documents. The codes selected through Match, Codes are not specific by value (such as a margin size or font size). You can, however, include the codes with text for the find process.

When you choose Type, Specific Codes, a Specific Codes dialog box appears. Any selection results in your further defining the find. For example, you won't just search for a Justification code, you will be asked to specify the type of justification such as Left. A limitation of specific code searches is that you can only find for one specific code at a time. You cannot combine the code with text (or other codes) for the find. These are the codes that can be made specific:

Bottom Margin	Font
Font Size	Horizontal Advance
Justification	Left Margin
Line Spacing	Left Margin Adjustment
Overstrike	Right Margin
Style	Right Margin Adjustment
Top Margin	Vertical Advance

Replacing Text

Replacing text is like finding except that it goes an extra step. You simply enter text and codes to Find, and those to Replace With. You will notice different command buttons on the Find and Replace dialog box that weren't on the Find Text dialog box. You may choose Find to find the text, then use Replace to replace the text. This way you can confirm each replacement. Or, you may choose Replace All to replace each occurrence of the text you want to find, without confirming. (Warning: Automatic replacements can be dangerous unless you are sure of what you are replacing.)

There are also a few Find and Replace Text alternatives that are different from the Find operation:

- Choose Direction, then choose Forward or Backward, to determine the direction of the search when replacing.

- Choose Options, Limit Number of Changes to limit the number of replacements made according to the Number you enter.

The following Quick Steps detail how to replace text.

Replacing Text

1. Select the text within which to search, if appropriate. Press Ctrl+F2, or select Replace from the Edit menu.

   The Find and Replace dialog box appears.

2. Enter the text and codes you want to find. (Use Match to control Whole Words and Case, or to find a Font or Code. Use Type, Specific Codes to specify codes with values.)

   You identify the text and/or codes to be found.

3. Enter the text and codes you want to Replace With.

   The text and/or codes that will be used in the replacement are identified.

4. Use Direction to identify whether to search Forward or Backward, and use Options to choose the extent of the search.

   The direction and extent of the search is determined.

5. Select Replace All to replace all occurrences of the text you want to find. Or select Find to find the first occurrence, then use Replace to complete the replacement (or choose Find again to leave the text and continue to the next occurrence).

Bookmarks

Bookmarks allow you to find a location in a document, regardless of the text or code the location contains. Bookmarks are especially helpful when you are working on large documents. One type of bookmark is a *QuickMark*. It is a fast way to enter a bookmark, but there can be only one QuickMark in a document.

To enter a QuickMark, put the insertion point in the appropriate spot. Press Ctrl + ⇧Shift + Q. The **Bookmark:QuickMark** code is placed in your document. To find a QuickMark from anywhere in your document, press Ctrl + Q.

You can have multiple bookmarks in a document besides the QuickMark, but each must have a unique name. With your insertion point where you want the bookmark to appear, choose Bookmark from the Insert menu. Select Create. The text immediately following the insertion point appears. Enter a Bookmark Name and choose OK. The bookmark is placed in your document.

To find a bookmark code, press F2 and find the Bookmark code. To find a specific bookmark, select Bookmark from the Insert menu. Highlight the bookmark to find, and select Go To.

Hypertext

Another twist on finding text involves using *hypertext*. Hypertext is text (typically a word or phrase) you identify to link parts of your document to the same document, another document, or to a macro that executes keystrokes and commands automatically. The uses of hypertext are ample. Here are a couple of examples to start you thinking. You can jump to reference materials to provide your reader with additional information. You can develop instructions to complete forms, and run automated forms set up in macros. (To learn more about macros, see Chapter 14, "Automating with Macros.")

First, create a link by identifying an existing Bookmark or macro to use with the hypertext. Second, mark the characters as hypertext. Then, set up a link from the hypertext to jump to the Bookmark or to run the macro. When you create a hypertext link, you can choose from these selections:

Go to **Bookmark:** To go to a bookmark in the current document.

Go to Other **D**ocument or Go to Other **B**ookmark: To go to another document, or a specified bookmark in another document.

Run Macro: To run a specified macro. The macro begins running at the hypertext location. If you want to leave the document containing the hypertext, you'll need to build the exit activities into the start of your macro.

You can also identify how you want the hypertext to appear. If you select Text, the hypertext text is highlighted. If you select Button, a button appears.

To create a hypertext link, follow these Quick Steps.

Create a Hypertext Link

1. Using F8 or the mouse, select the text to use as hypertext.

The hypertext is identified.

2. Select Hypertext from the Tools menu.

The Hypertext Feature Bar appears.

3. Select Create.

The Create Hypertext Link dialog box appears.

4. Identify the Hypertext Action (where to link to), and the Hypertext Appearance (Text or Button), and select OK.

A code appears in the document. Repeat steps 1 through 4 to set up as many links as you want.

5. Select Close when all links are set up.

You are returned to your document.

If you plan on using multiple hypertext links, make your hypertext *active* first. That way, you can press ® or click on the hypertext to jump to the link. To activate hypertext, select **H**ypertext from the **T**ools menu. The Hypertext Feature Bar appears. Choose the **A**ctivate button. (The option to De**a**ctivate appears while Hypertext is active.)

If you only want to make one jump, it may be faster to not make hypertext active. Put the insertion point on the hypertext. Select Hypertext from the Tools menu. On the Feature Bar, choose Perform.

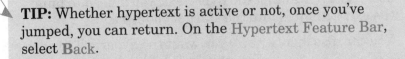

TIP: Whether hypertext is active or not, once you've jumped, you can return. On the Hypertext Feature Bar, select Back.

The Hypertext dialog box can be used for other activities. With the insertion point on your hypertext, you can choose Edit to change the link or format. Delete can be used to delete the link of the hypertext the insertion point rests on, or to delete all links in blocked text.

Comments

Finally, there is a twist on placing (and later finding) information in your documents. You can use *comments*. These appear in a text box on your screen, but are not printed.

To enter a comment, place the insertion point where you want the comment to appear. Select Comment from the Insert menu. Select Create, and add the text. From the Comment Feature Bar, choose Initials, Name, Date, and Time if you want any of those included in the comment. (Initials and Name must be set up through File, Preferences, Environment before using.) When you are done with the comment, choose Close. The text appears in a box, and a code is inserted.

To hide comments, choose Preferences from the File menu, choose Display, then deselect Comments. To display comments that are hidden, follow the same steps but make sure the check box for Comments is checked.

Arranging Document Windows

1. Select the Window menu.
2. Select Tile or Cascade.

Switching Between Document Windows

- To move between windows, select the window from the Window menu.
- Click on the window with the mouse.

Managing Files

1. From an appropriate dialog box (such as Open File), select the drive, directory, and file(s).
2. Select File Options, then Copy, Move, Rename, or Delete.

Creating a New Directory

1. From an appropriate dialog box (such as Open File), select File Options.
2. Choose Create Directory.
3. Enter the New Directory drive, path, and name, then select Create.

Finding a File with QuickFinder

1. From an appropriate dialog box (such as Open File), select QuickFinder.
2. Complete the criteria for the search, and select Find.

Chapter 13

Managing Documents

Experienced WordPerfect for Windows users are not the only ones who need to manage multiple documents; even beginners can benefit from WordPerfect's file-handling and retrieval capabilities. In this chapter, you'll learn some basic skills for managing your documents, both on-screen and on disks.

Working with Document Windows

Opening several documents at a time has a variety of benefits. You can have several documents readily available for reference or notes, or copy or move text between documents. WordPerfect creates a new *window* for each document you open.

For example, let's say you need to copy the heading information from the document called BENLET.WPD into a document you'll call BENLET2.WPD. Figure 13.1 shows the heading information in BENLET.WPD, and a yet-to-be-named document called "Document 2." Because BENLET.WPD is the active window (where the insertion point resides), the window's Title bar is darker. After selecting an appropriate block of text and then copying it, you place the text in another window—that is, Document 2. Notice that in Figure 13.2, BENLET2.WPD has been saved.

Figure 13.1
BENLET.WPD and Document 2.

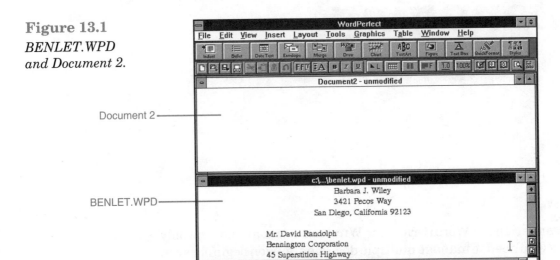

Figure 13.2
BENLET2.WPD created by copying BENLET.WPD contents to Document 2, then saving the document.

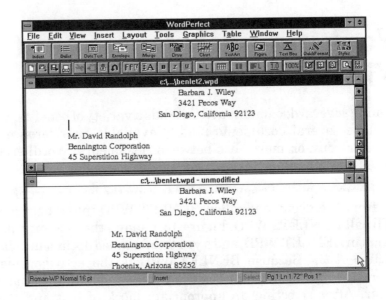

Opening and Closing Document Windows

To create a window, select File, New (or Ctrl+N) to open a new, blank windows. Or, select File, Open (Ctrl+O) from the File menu, and select an existing file to open into a window. To close a window, just close the document with File, Close, or exit WordPerfect for Windows.

Moving and Sizing Document Windows

As shown in Figure 13.3, the frame for a window has the Title bar with the title of the document at the top. You can use the keyboard or mouse to control the frame. We'll look at keyboard options first.

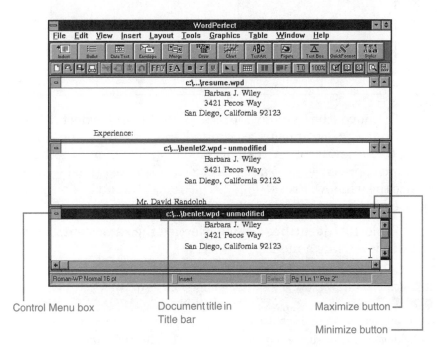

Control Menu box

Document title in Title bar

Maximize button

Minimize button

Figure 13.3
A window frame.

You can minimize the size of the window or maximize it. Press Alt + - to access the Control Menu box. Then select Minimize or Maximize. (Figure 13.4 shows a window minimized to icon size.) To enlarge a document that has been minimized to an icon, just double-click on the icon.

Figure 13.4
A window minimized to an icon.

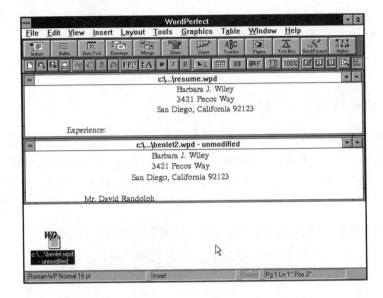

To move the window, press Alt + - and select Move. The window frame appears as a dotted line. Use the arrow keys to move to the new location, then press ⏎Enter. To change the size of a window, press Alt + - and select Size. Use the ↑ and ← keys to size the window. Press ⏎Enter. The Control Menu box may also be used to Close the window (or press Ctrl + F4).

Table 13.1 identifies how to exercise the same control over the window using a mouse.

Table 13.1
Controlling the Window Frame with the Mouse

Action	Result
Clicking on the Minimize button	Minimizes the window
Clicking on the Maximize button	Maximizes the window
Clicking on the Restore button	Restores the window after minimizing or maximizing

Action	Result
Dragging the Title bar	Moves the window
Dragging any side	Sizes the window
Double-clicking on the Control Menu box	Closes the window

TIP: You may use the **W**indow menu to switch to another window. Just select Window, then check the name of the document window you want. That document window becomes active.

Copying and Moving Step by Step

Whether you are working with full-screen displays or multiple windows on one screen, the method of copying or moving text is the same. Create the necessary windows, then select the text to copy or move. To cut (move), select Edit, then Cut (or press Ctrl+X). To copy, select Edit, then Copy (or press Ctrl+C). Place the insertion point in the window and location you want to cut or copy to. Complete the cut or copy by selecting Edit, then Paste (or press Ctrl+V). It's that simple.

Arranging Windows

Because you can open multiple windows at once, the screen can get messy. Plus, all windows may not appear on a single screen.

To arrange all your windows on one screen, select the Window menu, then select Tile or Cascade. Figure 13.5 shows several windows arranged using Tile. Figure 13.6 shows the same windows organized using Cascade.

Figure 13.5
Windows in a Tile arrangement.

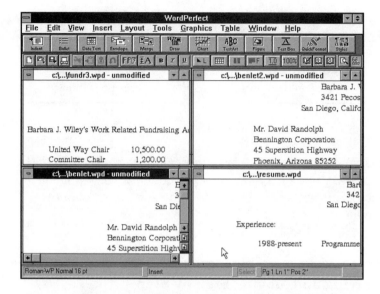

Figure 13.6
Windows in a Cascade arrangement.

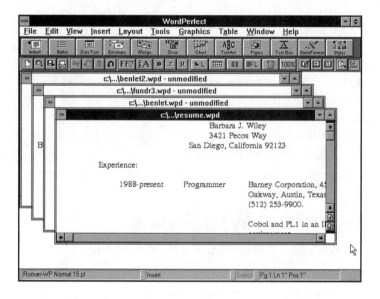

Switching Among Windows

To move from one window to another, select the Control Menu box with ⌊Alt⌋+⌊-⌋. Then select Next (or simply press ⌊Ctrl⌋+⌊F6⌋) to activate the next window. If you are using a mouse, you can click on any part of the window you want to activate. When you activate a window, the Title bar is colored or shaded, and your insertion point is active in the window.

CAUTION

If you retrieve the same document into two win-dows, and then edit one of the windows, the edits are not applied automatically to the document in the second window. If you make edits you want to keep, make sure they are made in one document, and that you have that document saved under the appropriate name. When you work with the same document in both windows, keep careful track of which document is the "latest and greatest" to save.

Managing Documents on Disks

When you start using WordPerfect for Windows, you'll have only a few documents, so managing them is easy. But as you create more documents, you may forget their names or contents—just locating the document you want can be a problem. Therefore it's important to have a system for managing your documents.

Following a scheme for naming documents is important so you can identify them readily. If, after creating several documents, you think of a better naming scheme, go ahead and rename the documents. Another important management task is to delete unnecessary documents so you can locate the useful ones easily. This section covers speedy file-management procedures that can help you get started with these important tasks.

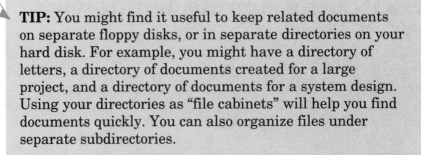

TIP: You might find it useful to keep related documents on separate floppy disks, or in separate directories on your hard disk. For example, you might have a directory of letters, a directory of documents created for a large project, and a directory of documents for a system design. Using your directories as "file cabinets" will help you find documents quickly. You can also organize files under separate subdirectories.

A Word About Directories and Subdirectories

To control your files, you need to be familiar with the concepts of directories and subdirectories. Appendix A includes more detail, but we'll hit the highlights here.

Basically, your hard disk can be divided into sections of any size called *directories*. These sections help you organize your files by use. For example, the WPWIN60 directory contains WordPerfect for Windows system files. The WPDOCS subdirectory was created when WordPerfect was installed, and is intended to contain document files. The *path* (which we've referred to earlier in this book) is a way to identify to your computer how to get to a particular directory, subdirectory, or file. For example, this path indicates the location of a letter called BENLET.WPD. It is stored on drive C, in the WPDOCS directory:

C:\WPWIN60\WPDOCS\BENLET.WPD

Managing Files

WordPerfect for Windows doesn't include a File Manager because the *directory dialog boxes* include all the requirements for managing files. Of these, the Open File dialog box is most useful. Don't be misled by the name. You can use this dialog box to do much more than just open files. The Open File dialog box is accessed through File, Open, or by pressing Ctrl+O. The Save As, Insert File, Insert Image, and other dialog boxes have some or all of the file-management features covered in the rest of this chapter; the Open File dialog box (shown in Figure 13.7) will be the example.

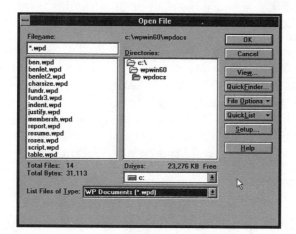

Figure 13.7
The Open File dialog box.

Locating a File or Files

To locate a file, type in (or select) the drive, path, and file identifier you want. For example, you could type in A:*.WPD in the Filename text box, then press ↵Enter. All the files on the disk in drive A that have the .WPD extension would be displayed.

TIP: If you type in a path that is not recognized, a message is likely to appear, saying you've entered an invalid drive or path. Check the punctuation you've used in the path—as well as the validity of the directories and filename you've used—carefully. Usually, some typographical error has occurred.

If you don't know the drive or directory you want to select, select Drives and Directories on the dialog box as needed. Select the drive and directory you want. If you want to list files of a certain type, use the List Files of Type command, and select the type from the drop-down list.

Once you have selected the drive and directory—along with the type of file—the Filename list for the files in that drive and directory will appear.

As mentioned, you may find a file in a directory by typing in the name of the file and pressing ⏎Enter. Another option is to use a *wildcard* (a special "shortcut" character) in place of part or all of the filename. Use an asterisk (*) to stand for multiple characters or a question mark (?) to stand for a single character. To see (for example) all the files that start with **W** and end with the file extension **WPD**, you could type in **W*.WPD** in the Filename text box.

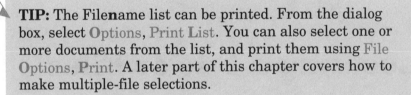

TIP: The Filename list can be printed. From the dialog box, select Options, Print List. You can also select one or more documents from the list, and print them using File Options, Print. A later part of this chapter covers how to make multiple-file selections.

Changing the Setup

The Setup button lets you change the way directory and file information is displayed. When you select Setup on the Open File dialog box, for example, the Open/Save As Setup dialog box appears. (As the name of this latter dialog box implies, you may also access it through the Save As dialog box.) Figure 13.8 illustrates the Open/Save As Setup dialog box.

Figure 13.8
The Open / Save As Setup dialog box.

Complete the File List Display to identify the amount of information you want to Show from that drop-down list. For example, in Figure 13.8, the file list will display the filename, the size of the file in bytes (a byte is approximately 1 character), and the date and time the file was last saved. You may use Sort By to select how filenames are sorted (by filename, for example, or by date and time). Finally, you can select the Sort Order (Ascending or Descending).

To keep as permanent the file list you have chosen to display, check Change Default Directory. In addition to keeping the "show" selections permanent, this method is also the way to set a new default directory for display.

Figure 13.9 shows the Filename list shown by Filename, Size, Date, and Time. It has been sorted by Date/Time, in Descending order.

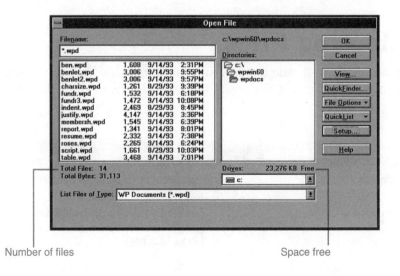

Figure 13.9
The Open File dialog box after changing Setup options.

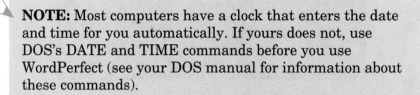

NOTE: Most computers have a clock that enters the date and time for you automatically. If yours does not, use DOS's DATE and TIME commands before you use WordPerfect (see your DOS manual for information about these commands).

In Figure 13.9, the number of files identified in the File**n**ame list appears. When you select files later for some other operation, this information is replaced with the number of files selected, and the total bytes selected. The remaining amount of free space (in bytes) is also shown.

NOTE: A *byte* is approximately equal to one character.

CAUTION   Never allow the free space to dwindle to less than 10% of the total space on your drive. If space becomes scarce, move documents to another disk, or delete unneeded documents.

Selecting Files

You can work with one document or several. Use the techniques in Table 13.2 to select files (one or multiple) from the File**n**ame list.

Table 13.2
Selecting Files
with the Keyboard
and the Mouse

To select files with the keyboard:	
Single file	Highlight the file with the arrow keys.
Files in order	Highlight the first file, hold down ⇧Shift), and use arrow keys to move to the last file.

To select files with the keyboard:	
Files out of order	Press ⬆Shift+F8, highlight the first file, press the Spacebar, highlight the second file, press the Spacebar, continue, and press ⬆Shift+F8 to end the selection.
Select all files	Press Ctrl+/ (forward slash).
Deselect all files	Press Ctrl+\ (backslash).

To select files with the mouse:	
Single file	Click on the file.
Files in order	Click on the first file, hold down ⬆Shift, and click on the last file.
Files out of order	Hold down Ctrl and click on each file.

Copying Documents

You will want to copy documents to create *backups*, in case a document becomes damaged or lost. One way to copy a document is to save it under another name, or to save it to another disk. You may also copy documents using dialog boxes. The benefits of this procedure are that you can copy a file on disk (instead of having to retrieve it to your screen), and you can copy more than one document in a single operation.

The following Quick Steps identify how to copy documents.

Copying One or More Document Files

QUICK
STEPS

1. From the dialog box (such as Open File), change the drive, path, and file information, if you want, and press ⏎Enter.

The file(s) available to copy appear.

continues

continued

2. Select each filename you want to copy. Then select File Options, Copy.

The Copy File(s) dialog box appears.

3. Enter the drive and path of the disk to which you want to copy the files. If you want to be prompted when an existing file has the same name, check Don't replace files with the same size, date, and time. Select Copy.

The file(s) are copied.

4. If you checked Don't replace files with the same size, date, and time and a file with the same name exists, select Copy to complete the copy.

Moving Documents

When you *move* a file, it is removed from the current disk location, and placed at a new location you have indicated. For example, you might move a file from one disk to another when the original disk is getting full, or if you want to sort the files on a disk you use less often.

CAUTION   Don't confuse moving a file with copying a file. When you *move*, the original location of the file is lost. When you *copy*, the original location of the file is preserved, and a duplicate of the file is made.

The following Quick Steps identify how to move documents.

Moving One or More Document Files

1. From the dialog box (such as Open File), change the drive, path, and file information, if you want, and press ↵Enter.

   The file(s) available to move appear.

2. Highlight each filename you want to move. Then select File Options, Move.

   The Move File(s) dialog box appears.

3. Enter the drive and path of the disk to which you want to move the files. Select Move.

   The file(s) are moved.

Renaming a Document

When you *rename* a document, the existing name is replaced with the new name you suggest. Renaming is useful when you determine a better way to organize existing files. For example, you may have created these three versions of a document:

DEARPT.WPD

DREPORT.WPD

DRT.WPD

You could rename these files to suggest the order in which they were created:

DERPT1.WPD

DERPT2.WPD

DERPT3.WPD

The following Quick Steps identify how to copy documents.

Renaming Document Files

QUICK STEPS

1. From the dialog box (such as Open File), change the drive, path, and file information, if you want, and press ⏎Enter. You can also select multiple files to rename.

The file(s) available to rename appear.

2. Highlight the single file you want to rename. Then select File Options, Rename.

The Rename File(s) dialog box appears.

3. Enter the new name (and drive and path, if different) in the To text box. Select Rename.

The file is renamed.

Deleting Documents

Deleting a document is useful when you are sure you will not want that version of the document again. For example, let's say you've created several different versions of BENLET.WPD for internal review. When you finalize one version, you may want to delete the other versions. This not only saves space, but saves possible future confusion about which version was used.

CAUTION When deleting, always proceed carefully. Check and double-check the file you want to delete, to make sure you will never again want the document. Once a document is deleted, it cannot be recovered through WordPerfect for Windows.

The following Quick Steps explain how to delete one or more files.

Deleting One or More Files

1. From the dialog box (such as Open File), change the drive, path, and file information, if you want, and press `Enter`.

   The file(s) available to delete appear.

2. Highlight the file(s) you want to delete. Then select File Options, Delete.

   The Delete File(s) dialog box appears, listing the File to Delete—or, if mutiple files are chosen, with a message like:

   Do you want to delete the selected file(s)?

3. Select Delete.

   The file(s) is immediately deleted.

Creating and Removing Directories and Subdirectories

You can create a new directory or subdirectory to store the files you have saved (or are about to save).

Decide on the drive, path, and unique name for the new directory. From the dialog box (such as Open File), select File Options, Create Directory. The Create Directory dialog box appears. Enter the drive, path, and name of the new directory. Make sure to enter backslashes (\) as appropriate. Select Create. The directory is created.

TIP: Once you have created a new directory, you can confirm its creation by looking at the **D**irectories list.

Here are the steps for deleting a subdirectory. From the dialog box, select the directory you want to remove. Then select File Options, Remove Directory. Confirm that the directory to delete is in the **D**irectory to Remove text box. Choose Remove. The directory is immediately deleted. If there are files in the directory, a message appears, indicating there are files and asking you to confirm the removal. If you continue, both the directory and all the files in it are deleted.

Using QuickFinder to Find a File

The capability of finding a file by filename (or a word in a file) is invaluable. The QuickFinder gives you this power.

Choose QuickFinder from the dialog box. The QuickFinder dialog box (like that shown in Figure 13.10) appears.

Figure 13.10
The QuickFinder dialog box.

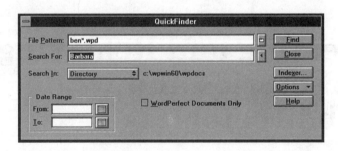

You may enter a File Pattern. (In Figure 13.10, all files with **BEN*.WPD** will be searched.) You may also enter specific text to Search For. In the figure, files with the word **Barbara** will be identified. Where to search is identified via the Search In drop-down list. (In Figure 13.10, the directory

C:\WPWIN60\WPDOCS will be searched.) Finally, you may check WordPerfect Documents Only to search only WordPerfect documents. To be selected, a file must meet all the criteria on the QuickFinder dialog box. When the criteria are entered, select Find.

While the search is underway, the Searching dialog box appears. It displays the directory and filenames as they are searched as well as the number of files which have been found. Once the search is complete, the Search Results List dialog box appears (see Figure 13.11).

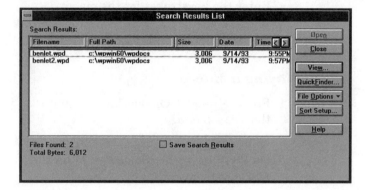

Figure 13.11
The Search Results List dialog box.

From the Search Results dialog box, you may use all typical file-related procedures—including viewing a file, copying a file, moving a file, and so on.

Recording a Macro

1. Press Ctrl+F10. Or select Macro and Record from the Tools menu.
2. Enter the Location, if necessary.
3. On the Record Macro dialog box, enter a Name and select Record.
4. Enter the keystrokes for the macro.
5. When done, press Ctrl+F10. Or select Macro and Record from the Tools menu.

Playing a Macro

1. Press Alt+F10. Or select Macro and Play from the Tools menu.
2. Enter the Location, if necessary.
3. On the Play Macro dialog box, enter the Name and select Play.

Editing a Macro

1. Select Macro and Edit from the Tools menu.
2. Enter the Location, if necessary.
3. On the Edit Macro dialog box, enter the Name and select Edit.
4. To finish, choose Save & Compile. When the macro is successfully saved, choose Close.

Automating with Macros

In this chapter, you will learn how to automate your activities to save time and effort. With an investment of just a little time, you'll discover a slick way to make WordPerfect for Windows perform tasks specific to your own needs—automatically.

Macros: Why and When

A *macro* stores your keystrokes and commands. Any time you want to replay the contents of the macro, just call it up with one or a few keypresses, and the rest is automatic.

When can you use a macro? There are plenty of opportunities. You may want to create a macro to type in your return address automatically, or your name, or other names and addresses you commonly use. You may want to use a macro to store formatting codes you use frequently. For example, if you often create letters with 1.5-inch margins and with justification off, you can enter those commands *once* in a macro, and then replay them in any document.

Another good use of macros is to store your common headers or footers. You can have a macro that stores all the keystrokes required to create a header or footer, or a macro that stores the keystrokes needed to exit the header or footer.

Macros save time. By placing header or footer activities in a macro, you save yourself from trying to remember exactly how you set up the header or footer the last time. Without the macro, you might find yourself looking for old documents—wasting time rummaging through files. In addition, macros save you from extra keyboard activity.

How do you know what macros to create? That's easy. Just watch what you do. Pay attention to activities you perform over and over—especially those that seem tedious, and those that could be faster or more pleasant if you let WordPerfect do them for you. Since virtually any WordPerfect keystrokes can be in a macro, your only limits are your imagination and your mastery of the steps for creating and using macros.

Don't Reinvent the Wheel

If you work in an office, other people may have created macros they're willing to share. Set up some means to pool macros with others in the office. You may want to go so far as to identify common naming conventions, and encourage very precise descriptions. Create a master list of macros and their descriptions, along with where to access the macros. Make this list available to everyone. If you work on a network, this list can be kept up to date in a document to which everyone has access.

Some work environments have one or two "macro masters" who have become expert at developing time-saving macros, and are willing to share their expertise. Find these people and set up a means by which everyone can benefit from their skill.

Recording a Macro

The easy way to get started using macros is to create one by entering keystrokes and recording them as you go. Creating a macro in this way is referred to as *recording* the macro.

Let's look at an example. Suppose you make frequent use of your return address centered on the page. A macro is a good way for you to store and replay the text.

To create the macro, press Ctrl+F10 or select Macro then Record from the Tools menu. The Record Macro dialog box appears. First, check the location where the macro will be saved by selecting Location. You may choose a location, including:

- Current Template or Default Template: Either of these choices will attach the macro to a special template for documents. The template can also include formatting settings for documents. Once you select a template option, the current macros used for the template appear on the Record Macro dialog box.

- File on Disk: This choice puts the macro in a separate macro file on disk, with the extension WCM. Once you are back on the Record Macro dialog box, you can access existing macros for the drive and directory by selecting the File button after the Name text box.

- Current Document: This choice assigns the macro to the current document.

- New Document: This choice assigns the macro to a new document to be created.

Once the location is selected, select OK.

Back on the Record Macro dialog box, enter a name in the Name text box for a macro to be assigned to a template or a file. (You will later enter this name when you want to use the macro.) To name a macro, type in eight or fewer letters. You don't include an extension with macros. WordPerfect takes care of that. Do use a descriptive name. Our example might be called **BRETADD** for Barbara's **RET**urn **ADD**ress. If you accidentally enter a name for a macro that you've already used, a message like this appears:

Macro BRETADD already exists, replace it?

Choose Yes or No.

After entering the name for the macro you are recording, select Record. The following prompt appears in the center of the window, at the bottom:

Macro Record

This reminds you that any keystrokes you enter will be placed in the macro.

Type in the text, and the appropriate WordPerfect for Windows key combinations. You can use most WordPerfect keyboard and mouse editing capabilities. (You cannot use a mouse, however, to position the insertion point within a macro.)

As you enter the keystrokes, you might make a typographical error or press an incorrect command. If you make a mistake that you can correct, first finish the macro keystrokes. WordPerfect for Windows corrects simple mistakes for you in the macro. Or, if it is a mistake WordPerfect doesn't pick up, you can either use the macro with the mistake and its correction (if no harm is done), or you can edit the macro contents (a procedure covered later in this chapter). An example of a mistake WordPerfect for Windows will correct is typing in this text when recording a macro:

San Dieb

To correct, you'd press Backspace to get to:

San Die

Then you'd complete the correct keystrokes before continuing:

San Diego

Once the macro text is entered, just press Ctrl+F10, or deselect Macro, Record from the Tools menu.

The following Quick Steps summarize the process of recording a macro.

Recording a Macro

1. Press Ctrl+F10, or select Macro, and then Record from the Tools menu.

   The Record Macro dialog box appears.

2. Select the Location, enter the macro location you want to record to, then select OK.

   The macro location is identified.

3. On the Record Macro dialog box, type in an eight-character (or less) name. Select Record.

   This message appears on the bottom of the screen: **Macro Record**.

4. Enter the keystrokes for the macro. When done, press Ctrl+F10. Or deselect Macro, Record from the Tools menu.

   Macro Record disappears, and you are returned to WordPerfect for Windows editing.

TIP: As you record the macro, you may want to pause the recording to check out certain WordPerfect for Windows features or perform a different task. You can do this by selecting Macro, Pause from the Tools menu. The message **Record Pause** appears at the bottom of the window. When you want to return to recording, make sure WordPefect for Windows is in the exact state it was when you paused. Select Macro, Pause from the Tools to remove the check mark. Continue recording the macro.

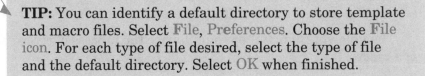

TIP: You can identify a default directory to store template and macro files. Select File, Preferences. Choose the File icon. For each type of file desired, select the type of file and the default directory. Select OK when finished.

As you create macros, it can be useful to keep your own list of macro names, descriptions, and uses. That way you can easily remember the use of each macro.

Playing a Macro

Once you have recorded a macro, you can use it. This is called *playing* a macro. (Breathe easy. The work's in the recording, not the playing.)

It is a good practice to play a new macro right after you've recorded it, to see whether it works the way you intended. If it doesn't, you can record it again, or edit the macro (as described later in this chapter).

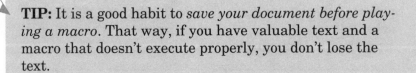

TIP: It is a good habit to *save your document before playing a macro*. That way, if you have valuable text and a macro that doesn't execute properly, you don't lose the text.

The following Quick Steps show how to play a macro.

Playing a Macro

1. Position the insertion point where the macro should play, and press Alt+F10. (Or select Macro and Play from the Tools menu.)

The Play Macro dialog box appears.

2. Change the Location, if required.	The macro you want to play is located.
3. Enter the macro name, and select Play.	The macro keystrokes are played.

Editing a Macro

To edit a macro, select Macro, then Edit from the Tools menu. From the Edit Macro dialog box, select the name of the macro, and select Edit. A display like that shown in Figure 14.1 appears. All the keystrokes appear, and each WordPerfect for Windows command appears. For example, the Center command (⇧Shift+F6) appears as **Center**, and a press of the ⏎Enter key appears as **HardReturn**. Text you have typed in appears after the word **Type**, in parentheses and curly brackets, with the text in quotes. For example, Barbara J. Wiley's name appears as:

Type ({"Barbara J. Wiley"})

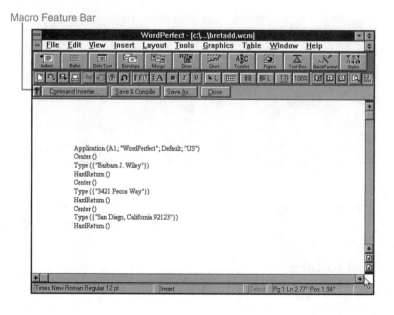

Macro Feature Bar

Figure 14.1
Edit Macro screen.

When editing, the Macro Feature Bar appears. The buttons on the *Feature Bar* are shortcuts for the editing process.

You may add or change commands or text. Just make changes to the macro file the way you would for any other WordPerfect document. (You must, however, make changes to the file in the form WordPerfect understands—including typing in commands and text.)

The *syntax* of a command refers to the form in which a command or text must be entered if WordPerfect is to recognize the action to take. The easiest way to learn the syntax of a few commands is to record them, and then look at their appearance. As you do this, you'll see that different commands have different syntax.

When you are done editing the macro, choose Save & Compile from the Macro Feature Bar.

If you enter a command or text incorrectly, you won't be able to save the macro. Instead, you'll get a **WordPerfect Macro Facility - Syntax Error** dialog box (like that shown in Figure 14.2.)

Figure 14.2
WordPerfect Macro Facility - Syntax Error dialog box.

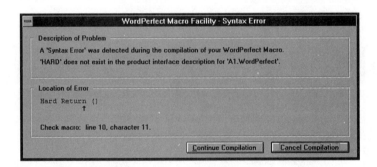

As shown in Figure 14.2, a description of the problem appears, along with identification of the line and character of the error. In the example, a Hard Return was entered as:

Hard Return

It should be entered as one word:

HardReturn

When it comes to identifying macro errors, WordPerfect isn't always perfect. The identification of the line is correct, but the character is off. Look at the whole macro when you consider problems. From the WordPerfect Macro Facility - Syntax Error dialog box, you may Continue Compilation to see other errors, or Cancel Compilation to return and fix the error identified.

Once you have saved the macro without errors, you may choose Close from the Macro Feature Bar. Play the macro once you have finished editing it, to make sure it works as you expect.

Data and Form Documents

- Data documents contain fields grouped in records. Use ⇧Shift+F9, **D**ata to create a data document. (You can also choose Tools, Merge, **D**ata.)
- Form documents contain boilerplate text and field codes. Use ⇧Shift+F9, **F**orm to create a form document. (You can also choose Tools, Merge, **F**orm.)

Merging Form and Data Documents

1. Press ⇧Shift+F9, **M**erge to merge form and data documents. (You can also choose Tools, Merge, **M**erge.)
2. Type in the name of the Form File, **D**ata File, and Output File. Complete other options, if you want.
3. Select OK.

Sorting a List

1. Press Alt+F9, or select Sort from the Tools menu.
2. Identify the Input File, **O**utput File, and other Sort options.
3. Select OK to start the sort.

Merging Documents and Sorting

WordPerfect for Windows allows you to *merge* the contents of one document with a list of data in another document. The data can comprise any small bits of information, such as names, addresses, telephone numbers, product numbers, sales regions, contributions, booth assignments, office numbers, birth dates, and so on.

If you ever need to send out form letters, or use the same data in multiple documents, the Merge feature will save you a great deal of time, and enable you to produce more personalized letters and documents. For example, you can create a list of names, addresses, and phone numbers of the members of a professional group, work team, or scout troop. Then you merge that data with a notice today, a letter tomorrow, or use it to make a list next week. Or you could create a document containing raw product data, and then pull out the data you need according to the requirements of the immediate document. Virtually any time you have a body of data that you will be using repeatedly, Merge is the way to go.

Elements of a Merge

Each piece of data in a merge is referred to as a *field*. A field may be a first name, last name, phone number, ZIP code—any single bit of information. All the related fields are organized into a *record*. For example, all the fields for one person (first name, last name, address, phone number) are organized into a record for that individual.

Three documents are involved in a merge:

- **The form file:** This is the *boilerplate* (that is, generic and reusable) text that will be used in the merged document. Type it in as regular WordPerfect for Windows text. In this document, you also identify what data you want plugged in. By entering codes for the fields, you tell WordPerfect what to put where.

- **The data file:** This document contains the data, organized in a way that lets WordPerfect for Windows identify what's what. For example, the fields in each record are listed in the same order, and the records are clearly separated. This way WordPerfect knows what type of field comes first, second, third, and so on. Also (just as importantly), WordPerfect knows where one record ends and another begins.

- **The merged document:** This is the result of merging the form and data documents. The data from the data document is entered at the appropriate spots, according to the instructions in the form document.

Let's take a look at an example of each type of document. We'll use Barbara Wiley's notice to the members of her professional group. Figure 15.1 shows the form document. Notice that each field to be inserted during the merge is identified:

FIELD(first name)

In the Reveal Codes screen, you'll see

MRG:FIELDfirst nameMRG:FIELD

that reminds you that the field is to be merged.

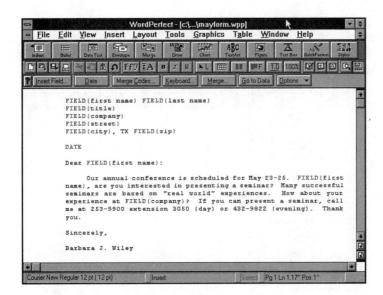

Figure 15.1
Form document.

Figure 15.1 illustrates that the order of the fields is not important. The numbers of the fields simply let WordPerfect for Windows match up with the proper data in the data document. Also, fields do not need to be represented an equal number of times in the form document: the first name is used three times and the company name is used twice.

Now let's take a look at the data document. Figure 15.2 shows the full screen display of two records. Notice that each field (such as first name) is entered on its own line, and ends with:

ENDFIELD

You can see that there are more fields in the data document than are called for in the form. The phone numbers, for example, appear in the data document, but are not used in the form document. This illustrates that you can use as much or as little data as you want.

Figure 15.2

Full-screen display of records in a data document.

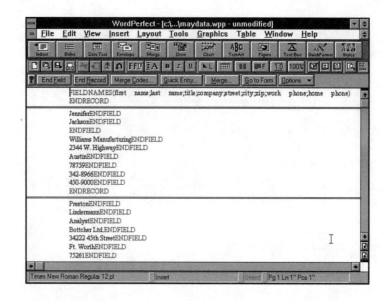

Take a look at the end of the record for Jennifer Jackson. The notation **ENDRECORD** signifies to WordPerfect that this record ends and the next record begins. (WordPerfect enters a hard page break for you, automatically.) The figure also shows that Jennifer Jackson's title is not available. A line is left as a placeholder to alert WordPerfect, but the **ENDFIELD** code is entered anyway.

Look at the order of the data in each record: the first name is always first, then the last name, title, company, and so on. The order in which your fields present data does not matter (for example, the last names could make up the first field). All records must have the fields in the same order by type, however, and the same number of field lines. When the merge code

FIELD(first name)

is in the form document, the first-name data is merged.

Figure 15.3 shows the codes as shown in the Reveal Codes screen. The code

MRG:ENDFIELD

marks the end of each field. The code

MGR:ENDRECORD

marks the end of each record. Notice that a hard page break **HPg** is also entered after the end of a record. The name of each field appears in the lower center of the window. (If you don't name the fields, WordPerfect assigns numbers. In this chapter, we'll cover how to name fields.)

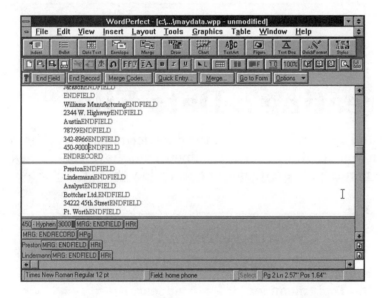

Figure 15.3
Data document Reveal Codes.

Figure 15.4 shows the first document (for Jennifer Jackson) fully merged, and it shows the beginning of the merging of the second document (for Preston Lindermann). The result of the merge, then, is one or more documents—with the applicable fields from each record in the data document merged into the form document. You can edit or print the merged document.

Figure 15.4
Merged documents.

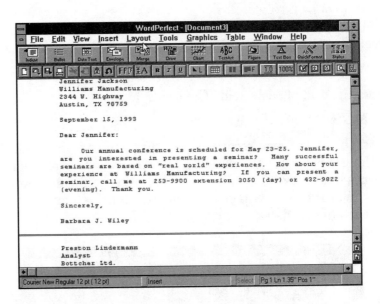

Creating a Data File

A sound approach is to create the data document first. That way, when you create the form document, you have established the field names in the data document. Follow these Quick Steps.

Creating a Data Document

1. Select Merge from the Tools menu (or press ⌂Shift+F9). — The Merge dialog box appears.

2. Select Data. — The Create Merge File dialog box appears.

3. Identify the window you want to use, and select OK. — The Create Data File dialog dialog box appears.

4. In the Name a Field text box, type in the first field name, and press ↵Enter. Continue until all field names are entered in order. Select OK.

The FIELDNAMES codes appear in your document, and you are taken to the Quick Data Entry dialog box.

5. Enter the data for the first field, and press ↵Enter.

The first field is entered.

6. Enter all the fields for a record following the process in step 5. When all fields are entered, select New Record.

The first record is entered followed by **ENDRECORD** then a hard page break.

7. Enter the fields for the next record. When you are done, select Close.

The last record is entered and a **Save changes to disk?** message appears.

8. Select Yes.

The Save Data File As dialog box appears.

9. Enter the drive, path, and Filename for the document and select OK.

The data document is complete.

TIP: If you need to add to or delete field names, just edit the field names between the codes to reflect the data in the file. Then save and exit the document, and retrieve it. The changes will have taken effect.

Before leaving the data document for good, check the field entries and the end of each record carefully. Answer these questions:

- Does each record have the same number of fields?

- Are the types of fields in the same order in each record?

- Is there an **ENDFIELD** code at the end of each field?

- Is there an **ENDRECORD** code at the end of each record (including the last record)?

- Are there unnecessary blank lines, spaces, or text that should be deleted?

CAUTION   When entering the "end field" and "end record" codes in an existing data document, do not type in **ENDFIELD** or **ENDRECORD**. You must use the appropriate WordPerfect menu selections. If you are adding or editing records, you may use the End Field and End Record buttons from the Command Bar to enter the appropriate codes.

FYI IDEAS

Saving Data Entry Time

Entering the "end field" and "end record" codes in an existing data document can become tedious. Also, some records may include similar information (such as addresses containing common city, state, and ZIP). To save time and reduce the tedium, use the Copy command.

Enter the sample record. Save the file. Select the sample record with F8 or the mouse. Use the Edit, Copy, then Edit, Paste commands to copy the record. Finally, go back and add or delete text in the records to meet your needs. The development of the document is simplified.

A more sophisticated approach is to create a macro. With some study, you can have the macro pause to allow you to enter field data.

Creating a Form File

To create a form file, press ⌐Shift⌐+⌐F9⌐ or select Merge from the Tools menu. Select Form. On the Create Merge File dialog box, identify whether you want to Use File in Active Window or create a New Document Window. Then select OK. On the Create Form File dialog box, enter the Associated Data File (or None if you have no data file). Select OK.

Enter text as you would in any WordPerfect document. When you want to enter a field to be filled in from the data file, select Insert Field. The Insert Field Name or Number dialog box appears. Select the field name you want inserted at the location of your insertion point, and choose Insert. The entry looks like this:

FIELD(first name)

Again, do not type in FIELD from your keyboard. If you do, that text will print, and you will not be calling data from the data document. You must use the WordPerfect keypresses or menu selections.

Continue typing in the boilerplate text and entering fields as you want. Fields need not be entered in order, and you can use all the fields in the data document, or only a few. When you are done creating the form document, save it as you would any other WordPerfect document.

Using Data Documents More Than Once

Don't forget that the information in data documents can be used for more than one form document. For example, you may have a customer list in a data document. One form document might be used to generate a form letter thanking customers for their business. Such a document would be for 8.5-by-11-inch letterhead. Another form document could be used to generate envelopes for the form letter. This form document would include the paper size/ type for envelopes. Another form document might create a

continues

continued

postcard-size sales notice. A form document would be needed to generate mailing labels to be used with the postcard. Need other ideas? How about customized holiday greetings for the customers on the list? As you can see, the use of form documents is limited only by your imagination.

The following Quick Steps summarize creating a form document.

QUICK STEPS

Creating a Form Document

1. Press Shift+F9 or select Merge from the Tools menu.	The Merge dialog box appears.
2. Select Form.	The Create Merge File dialog box appears.
3. Select Use File in Active Window or New Document Window and select OK.	The Create Form File dialog box appears.
4. Enter the Associated Data File or None and choose OK.	
5. Enter text and use the Insert Field button to insert fields as needed. When done, save the document with F3.	The form document is complete.

Be sure to check your document before saving, asking these questions:

- Have you entered each field with the correct number?
- Is the punctuation placed appropriately around the field data that will be inserted?

Merging

Once you have completed the form and data documents, you can merge them. Follow these Quick Steps.

Merging Documents

1. Press ⓈShift+F9 (or select Merge from the Tools menu).

   The Merge dialog box appears.

2. Select Merge.

   The Perform Merge dialog box appears.

3. Identify the Form File, Data File, and Output File.

   The files are identified.

4. Choose Options to ensure each merged document is separated with a page break, and that blank lines will be removed if there is no data in a data field. Select OK.

   You are returned to the Perform Merge dialog box.

5. Select OK.

   The merge begins.

TIP: The form file and data file are accessed from the disk; you must save the files and any edits. If you edit the documents on screen but do not save them, the changes will not be used in the merge.

TIP: If you want to create document pages to print envelopes during the merge, select Envelopes from the Perform Merge dialog box. On the Envelope dialog box, enter the Return Addresses (if desired). Enter the Mailing Addresses. Use the Field button to enter merge fields. The sample appears, available for you to alter fonts and envelope sizes. Select Options to shift the address positions.

Once the merge is complete, the merged documents appear on your screen, or in the document identified. Check to make sure the result is as you expected. Save the document. You can edit it and print it as you would any WordPerfect document.

You can use a database (or other files created with programs other than WordPerfect) for the data file. Select Spreadsheet/Database on the Insert menu. Select Import. On the Import Data dialog box, identify the Data Type (such as spreadsheet) and Import As Merge Data File. Identify the Filename, Named Ranges, and Range. Select OK. Check the document, and test it in a merge. Chapter 18, "Getting Information From and To Other Sources," describes importing in more detail.

When you begin using Merge, your first results may not come out as you want. This is pretty normal. Call up the data document, and check each record and field carefully. Then look at your form document, and check each field carefully. Pay special attention to the fields and records where the data did not print appropriately. After making corrections, try again.

Inserting the Current Date

WordPerfect has a variety of commands you can use for merging. The **D**ate command is especially helpful. Place it in your form document, and the current date will print in place of the code.

To use the date command:

1. Place your insertion point in the form document where you want the date placed.

2. Select the Date command button. **DATE** appears in the document where the date will print.

To see other merge codes, select Merge Codes. Figure 15.5 shows the Insert Merge Codes dialog box, with **DATE** highlighted.

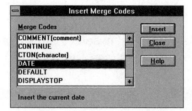

Figure 15.5
The Insert Merge Codes dialog box, with Date selected.

Sorting

WordPerfect for Windows allows you to *sort* lists alphabetically or numerically. This is particularly useful when creating a data-merge document. To sort, simply select the text you want to sort (if you don't make a selection, the contents of the entire document will be sorted). For example, Figure 15.6 shows a list to sort.

> Before you sort, always save a copy of your document. That way, if the result of the sort is different from what you imagined, you still have the original document to try the sort again.
>
> **CAUTION**

Figure 15.6
A list to sort.

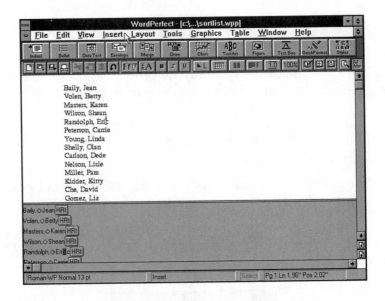

To sort, press Alt + F9 or select Sort from the Tools menu. The Sort dialog box appears (see Figure 15.7).

Figure 15.7
The Sort dialog box, for defining the sort.

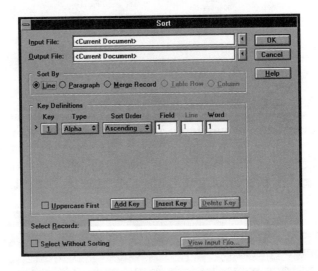

Enter the Input File (the source) and the Output File (the destination). For the Record Type, identify Line (to sort records that are a line in length), Paragraph (to sort records that are a paragraph long), Merge Record (to sort data merge records), Table Row (where each record is a row of cells), or Column (where each record is a row of columns).

Next, enter the Key Definitions. They specify which piece of the record you want to sort by first (Key 1), second (Key 2), and so on. For example, the criteria for sorting on Key 1 take precedence over those for Key 2. The Type indicates whether the characters to sort on are Alpha or Numeric. Next, the Order of sorting for the key can be Ascending (A to Z or 1 to 9) or Descending (Z to A or 9 to 1).

Identify the Field next. Fields in lines or paragraphs are separated by tabs or indents. Fields in merge records are separated by ENDFIELD codes, and those in table rows are separated into cells. Fields are considered to be numbered from left to right. Finally, identify the Word. Words are separated by spaces, forward slashes, and hard hyphens (and are also numbered from left to right within in the field).

For example, you can have a list of product-item numbers, the item's description, and its size in line records with two fields separated by tabs like this:

546890	Shirt/M
435677	Shirt/XL
435677	Shirt/M
435677	Shirt/S

The first Key to sort on (Key 1) could be the product-item number. To find this field and word for the sort, WordPerfect needs the following Key information. That is:

Key	Type	Sort Order	Field	Word
1	Numeric	Ascending	1	1

The product item is in the first field (there are two fields separated by tabs) and is the first and only word in the field.

The second Key to sort on (Key 2) is a little more tricky. We want to sort by size. The Key information is:

Key	Type	Sort Order	Field	Word
2	Alpha	Ascending	2	2

The Field is **2** because the first field in the record is the product number, and the second field is the product description and size. The fields are separated by a Tab. The Word is **2** because the product description (Shirt) is the first word. A forward slash separates it and the second word, which is the size (the word on which we want to sort).

The result of this sort would be as follows. The first key (the product number) is sorted first. Then, the size is sorted within each product number group.

435677	Shirt/M
435677	Shirt/S
435677	Shirt/XL
546890	Shirt/M

Once the Sort Keys are set up, if you want the result to be limited to records with certain criteria, you can enter values in the Select Records text box. For example, to sort only shirts that are Mediums (Key 2), enter the value **Key2=M**. If you enter selection criteria and decide to try the sort without the criteria, you can check Select Without Sorting.

Finally, you can check Uppercase First to put keys with uppercase letters before those with lowercase.

Once the Sort dialog box is complete, select OK to begin the sort.

The result of the name sort is shown in Figure 15.8. Notice that the lines were sorted in ascending alphabetical order. No code is placed in the document.

The following Quick Steps summarize how to sort a list.

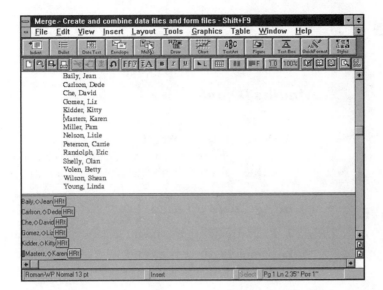

Figure 15.8
A sorted list.

Sorting a List

1. Press Alt + F9, or select Sort from the Tools menu.

   The Sort dialog box appears.

2. Enter the Input File and the Output File, then complete the Sort dialog box values, and select OK.

   The document is sorted.

Adding Default Lines

1. Position the insertion point.
2. Press Ctrl+F11 for a horizontal line or Ctrl+⇧Shift+F11 for a vertical line (or make either selection from the Graphics menu).

Adding Custom Lines

1. From the Graphics menu, select Custom Line.
2. Complete the entries and select OK.
3. To edit, select Graphics, Edit Line.

Adding Paragraph, Page, or Column Borders

1. From the Layout menu, select Paragraph, Page, or Column.
2. Select Border/Fill.
3. Complete the entries and select OK.

Creating a Text Box

1. Select Text from Graphics menu.
2. Complete the options on the Feature Bar.

Creating a Figure

1. Select Figure from the Graphics menu.
2. Enter the Filename of the figure, and select OK.
3. Complete the options on the Feature Bar.

16

Using Graphics in Your Documents

Whether you have a printer that handles sophisticated graphics, or you have a simple printer that produces basic results, there are graphic features you can use in your documents. This chapter will get you up and running.

NOTE: Not all printers handle all line and graph options. You will need to experiment to see what your printer can produce.

Adding and Editing Vertical and Horizontal Lines

WordPerfect is like the slogan from *The Outer Limits*, except that *"You* control the horizontal. *You* control the vertical."

You can add horizontal or vertical lines in your document for a pleasing effect. The lines can be black or a shade of gray, and you can set their width. For example, the sample résumé shown in Figure 16.1 is dressed up with horizontal and vertical lines. Even though no fancy fonts are used, the resumé is much more striking with the simple addition of lines.

Figure 16.1

A sample resumé with lines added.

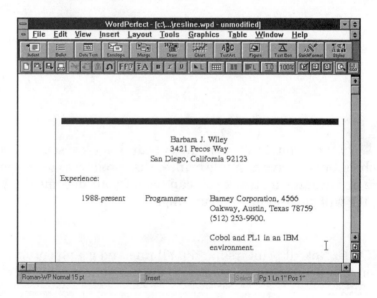

Adding a Line

Before adding lines or any graphic effects, always save a version of your document before you begin. That way, if the result is not as you anticipated, you can go back to your clean document. After you've saved your work, follow these Quick Steps to create a custom line.

Creating a Custom Line

1. Position your insertion point, and select Custom Line from the Graphics menu.

   The Create Graphic Line dialog box appears (Figure 16.2).

2. Select a Line Style.

   The Line Style appears in the sample.

3. For Line Type, choose whether you want to create a Horizontal or Vertical line.

4. Identify the Position/ Length of the line by entering the Horizontal and Vertical position of the line, from the top and left of the page, respectively. Enter the Length of the line.

   The sample is updated per your choices.

5. Enter the Spacing to maintain Above Line and Below Line.

   The sample is updated.

6. Change Color (if desired) by choosing a Line Color, or check Use Line Style Color to use the color shown in Line Color.

   To achieve gray tones, the Color can be a percentage of black. Not all printers handle color and gray shades. You may want to test yours.

7. Enter the Thickness of the line.

   Ensure the sample is as you like.

8. Select OK to return to your document.

   The line is created.

Figure 16.2

*The Create
Graphic Line
dialog box.*

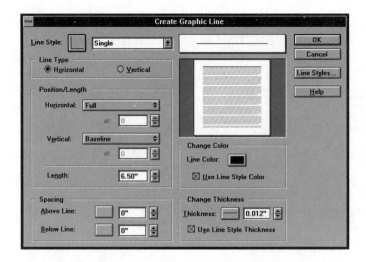

When you return to your document, it will have a code like the following placed in it:

Grph Line: Horz, Full, 6.50"

The code indicates whether the line is horizontal or vertical, its position, and its length.

The top horizontal line shown in the résumé in Figure 16.1 was set with the Line Style as Extra Thick Single, Line Type at Horizontal, Position at Horizontal Full and Vertical Baseline, Length at 6.50", Line Color as black.

The vertical lines in Figure 16.1 were set up with the Line Style Single, Line Type Vertical, Position Horizontal (for each vertical line) at Left Margin for one line and Right Margin for the other. For both lines, the Vertical Position was set to Top of page (extending from the top margin), and the Length at 9". Line Color was black.

TIP: There is a quick way to set up simple lines (with default rather than custom settings). Position your insertion point then choose Ctrl+F11 (or Graphics, Horizontal Line) or Ctrl+Shift+F11 (or Graphics, Vertical Line). Experiment with these lines. Don't forget to use View, Two Page to see full page images.

Editing a Line

Once you see the line on the page, you may realize that it needs some modification. Follow these Quick Steps.

Editing a Line

1. Place your insertion point before the code for the line.

   The Edit Graphic Line dialog box appears, with the values for the line.

2. Select Graphics, Edit Line.

   The Edit Graphic Line dialog box appears, with the values for the line.

3. Enter your changes, and select OK.

TIP: From Page and Two Page modes, you can move and size a line with the mouse. With the tip of the mouse pointer on the line, click on the line to select it. A dotted line with box handles appears around the line. You can drag the line to a new location, or use the handles on the line to enlarge or reduce it.

Paragraph, Page, and Column Borders

Want a border around the paragraph, page, or column? If so, WordPerfect has a special feature for you. You can place a border around a paragraph, page, or column, and enter *fill* (the shade inside the bordered area). Follow these Quick Steps.

Putting a Border on a Paragraph, Page, or Column

1. Select the Layout menu then Paragraph, Page, or Columns.

The Border/Fill option appears on the menu.

2. Select Border/Fill.

The Paragraph, Page, or Column Border dialog box appears.

3. Select a Border Style and a Fill Style. The Fill Style determines the shading on the page inside the border. For example, a 10% fill gives a light gray appearance. To customize the border's appearance further, select Customize Style, and make changes. Select OK.

A code, like this, appears in your document: **Pg Border**

To delete the border, delete the code. To stop the border from appearing later in the document, return to the Paragraph, Page, or Column Border dialog box. Set the Border Style option to None. (To turn off the border temporarily, choose Off in the dialog box.)

TIP: You may select text before setting the border. That way, the text you select will be surrounded by the border. For example, if you select two paragraphs on a page and then set a paragraph border, both paragraphs will be inside the border.

Graphics Boxes

A *graphic border* is simply a design placed around a word or paragraph (such as text) to dress it up. A *graphics box* is important—graphics boxes are WordPerfect's way of handling figures, equations, and other special graphic elements. WordPerfect for Windows places each special graphic element in its own box, so the element can be easily manipulated. You can also create a graphics box and put text in it, to lend your text the same flexibility of movement.

WordPerfect allows you to choose from different types of graphics boxes. In this chapter, we'll cover details about *text boxes* (designed to contain text) and *figure boxes* (which are useful for clip-art images, drawings, and charts).

The same Feature Bar is used for controlling text and figure boxes. It is shown in Figure 16.3.

As an overview, these are the options on the Feature Bar that you can control for boxes. (For a detailed walk-through of the text and figure boxes, read the next section of this chapter.)

- Caption: If you want a caption on the box, use this option to enter the text for it.

- Content: This option enables you to select the type of box contents (such as text or image). For example, if you are creating a figure box, look here for the path and name of the file containing the graphic. You may also edit text boxes.

Figure 16.3

The Feature Bar used with text and figure boxes.

Feature Bar——

- **P**osition: This option identifies how you want the box handled when the surrounding text is edited. Select Put Box on Current Page (Page Anchor) and the box will be kept on the specified page. Select Put Box in Current Paragraph (Paragraph Anchor), and the box will be kept with the surrounding text, even if you move the text. Choose Treat Box as Character (Character Anchor) for the box to be handled as a character on the line containing the insertion point. Enter the horizontal and vertical position (the options vary depending on the earlier setting).

- **S**ize: Here you identify how to set the width and height of the box. You can choose to set the width or height, have either one take up the full area, or have WordPerfect size the box according to its contents.

- **B**order/Fill: Here you identify the border style and the fill (shading) inside the box. You may select Customize Style to fine-tune the border and fill.

- **W**rap: Use this option to identify how you want text to wrap around the box or through the box. In some cases, you can choose Contour to have the text follow the shape of the graphic. It's a sophisticated look.

- Style: This option identifies the type of box.

- Tools: This option provides tools to edit graphics (though it's not available when you are creating a text box).

Enclosing and Editing Text in a Box

To see how to set up a box, we'll look at a *text box* first. Entering text in a box is good to emphasize it, or set it apart from the body of the text. Figure 16.4 shows a simple use of this feature.

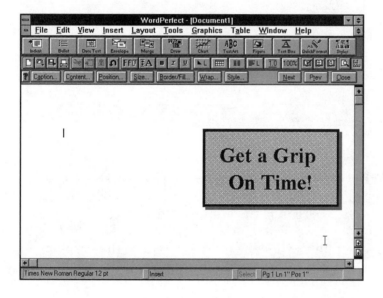

Figure 16.4

Text placed in a box.

Don't Forget Headers and Footers

A good use of text boxes is in headers or footers. Instead of simple text, a box around the text and shading can add interest.

To place text in a box, select Text from the Graphics menu. A text box appears which is selected (see Figure 16.5). Handles appear around a box when it is selected.

Figure 16.5

The text box when first created.

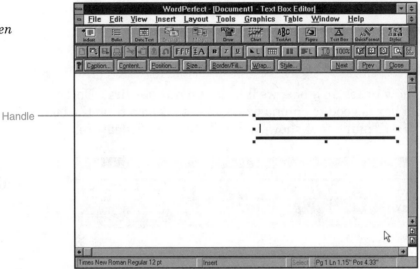

Handle

If you didn't intend to create a text box, you may select Style after selecting Text, and change the box style.

TIP: Use the mouse to move and size existing boxes. Click on the box. The box is selected, and a dotted line with handles surrounds the graphic. Once selected, you can drag the graphic to a new location. You can drag the handles on the line to enlarge or reduce the graphic.

Start working with the text box by sizing the box as desired. You may use the mouse to drag a handle on the existing box, or use Size to enter the sizing more precisely.

Next, identify the text content for the box. There are two ways to do this. The first way is to select Content, then Edit. The insertion point is placed in the box, and you may enter any text you like. Use any of WordPerfect for Windows editing capabilities, including fonts. The second way to identify the text the box will hold is to retrieve an existing file (by selecting Content, Filename) and enter the file's path and name.

Finally, you can make other selections to control the visual appearance of the text box. In the example, **B**order/Fill was selected. Thick Shadow was selected for the **B**order Style. The **F**ill Style was set at 20% fill to shade the interior of the box.

Before adding text outside of the box, check Wrap to make sure the text will wrap around (or through) the box as you desire. Because the text was allowed to flow around the box, we can type text around the text box. Figure 16.6 shows the document with text added outside the text box. Notice (in Reveal Codes) that there are no hard returns in the paragraph. Text just wraps around the text box.

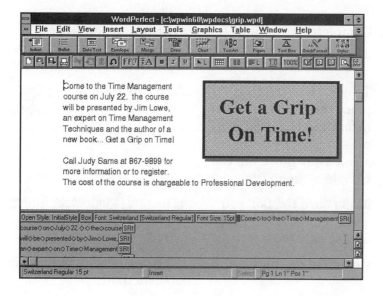

Figure 16.6
Text wrapped around the text box.

To delete a box, delete the code for the box. To edit the contents of a text box, select the box. Place your insertion point before the code for the box. Press ⬆Shift+F11 or select **E**dit Box from the Graphics menu. The Box Find dialog box appears. The box directly after the insertion point is identified. You may change the box you want to edit, or select OK. The box is selected for editing, and the Feature Bar appears. Make the changes.

Creating and Editing Text Boxes

Now that you've seen an example, the steps for creating a text box should make more sense. The following Quick Steps summarize how to create and edit a text box.

QUICK STEPS

Creating and Editing a Text Box

1. Select Text from the Graphics menu.

   A text box is immediately created at your insertion point, and the Feature Bar appears.

2. Complete the options.

   The box appearance changes as you change the options.

3. To edit the box later, place the insertion point before the box code, and press ⇧Shift+F11 (or select Edit Box from the Graphics menu).

   The Box Find dialog box appears.

4. Make sure the box you want to edit is identified, and select OK.

   The box is selected, and the Feature Bar appears.

5. Complete the options.

   The box is edited per your instructions.

Adding and Editing Figures

WordPerfect comes with a number of *graphics* you can insert into flyers, memos, newsletters, and so on. You can use the graphic files in virtually any document that calls for a little pizzazz.

While most printers will handle lines and text boxes, not all will print the graphics supplied with WordPerfect for Windows. Test your computer to see if this fancy feature will work for you.

Using or Creating Custom Graphics

You can use graphics from third-party sources, or create your own custom graphics with the Draw feature of WordPerfect for Windows (or with products like CorelDRAW!). This opens up a wide variety of effects and options. You can be very specific in designing your own letterhead, business cards, birthday cards, invitations, brochures, or advertisements.

Before you buy a graphics product, make sure it is compatible with WordPerfect. You can check your WordPerfect Reference for compatible file formats. Or you can check with the manufacturer of the product you are considering, to find out whether the product is compatible with WordPerfect.

If you try to use a graphic file that is incompatible, you may have luck using WordPerfect's *graphic conversion program* to convert the file to WordPerfect graphic format. Check your WordPerfect Reference for specific instructions on graphic file conversion.

Let's walk through adding a figure box. Select Figure from the Graphics menu. The Insert Image dialog box appears. Select a Filename, and enter the path and filename of the graphic you want to place in the figure. The graphics that come with WordPerfect for Windows end in WPG (for "WordPerfect Graphic"), and are shown in the list. In our example (see Figure 16.7), the HOTROD.WPG file was selected.

Figure 16.7

*The
HOTROD.WPG
file is selected.*

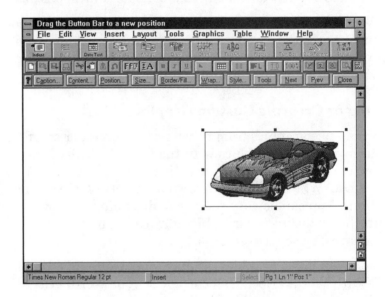

If the Feature Bar is not available, press ⇧Shift + F11. In the example, the figure was positioned with the mouse. **B**order/Fill was selected, and the **B**order Style was set to None. **W**rap was chosen, and the Wrapping Type was set to **C**ontour. Wrap Text Around was set to **B**oth Sides. Figure 16.8 shows the result after text was added.

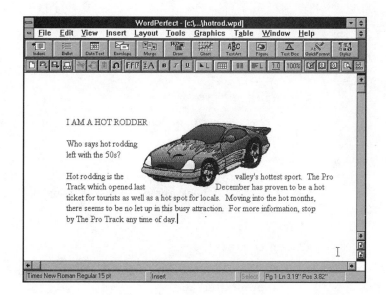

Figure 16.8
The figure with text added.

Creating a Style

1. Press ⌐Alt¬+⌐F8¬, or select Styles from the Layout menu.
2. Select Create.
3. Complete Style Name, Description, Type, and Contents. Check any check boxes desired. Select OK.

Using a Style

1. Position the insertion point or select text as appropriate.
2. Press ⌐Alt¬+⌐F8¬, or select Styles from the Layout menu.
3. Highlight the style you want, and choose Apply.

Style Contents and Control

- Styles can include codes, text, and graphics.

Creating and Using Styles

If you develop reports, newsletters, or other documents with special font, graphic, or text effects, you will want to learn about styles. Using styles allows you to save many keystrokes by automating common formatting options.

A *style* is usually thought of as a collection of formatting instructions that you identify on the basis of your own needs. You can also include graphics and text in a style, however, as well as formatting codes. Then use the style whenever you want to insert that set of codes, graphics, or text into your document. Styles save time (because you don't have to continually re-enter the formatting codes), and increase accuracy (because the style is tested, you know it is correct).

When should you create a style? Create a style for any special formatting, text, or graphics you use over and over. For instance, you can create company reports, develop organization newsletters, or create letters or memos with varied formatting elements. Using styles will speed the more repetitive tasks in developing such documents, and free you to concentrate on the more creative aspects of your work.

The real beauty of styles comes when you want to change a style. Suppose you have a 50-page document with multiple occurrences of a heading. Changing the style once affects all headings. If you had to enter the formatting manually or with a macro, each occurrence of the heading would have to be changed individually.

TIP: You can include in a style any codes, graphics, or text that can be put in a regular WordPerfect for Windows document. This includes figures, lines, names, addresses, special fonts, formatting, codes for indexes or tables of contents, column on and off settings, and so on.

The example in Figure 17.1 shows a monthly flyer describing company news. It includes five customized styles, with different fonts that account for the unusual spacing of text. The five styles created for this example are:

- **Flyer heading:** Includes the font codes, title of the flyer, and the solid line.

- **Major heading** for the body of the company flyer: Contains the font and underline codes.

- **Minor heading** for the flyer's body text: Contains the font.

- **Body** of the company flyer: Contains the font and tab codes.

- **Article divider** for the company flyer: Contains the line code.

Styles and Graphics

If you find yourself defining graphics options often, you may want to set up a style for each of the different option settings you use. This way, you will not have to redefine the options each time you want to switch. Just insert the new style, and away you go.

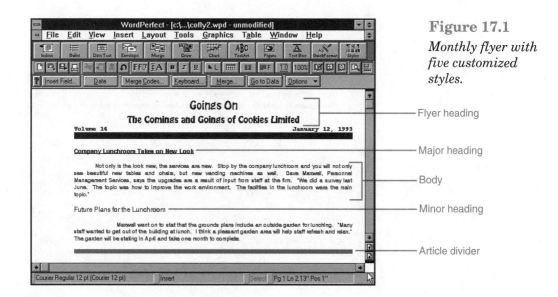

Figure 17.1
Monthly flyer with five customized styles.

Types of Styles

When you create and use a style, the style can be one of three types:

Paragraph Style (paired codes): Affects the paragraph at the insertion point, or in the text you've blocked.

Character Style (paired codes): Affects text that has been blocked, or text you are about to enter.

Document Style (open, single code): Affects all text from the insertion point to the end of the document.

Figure 17.2 shows character-style codes in place for the flyer. Because a *character style* creates paired codes, there is a code at the beginning and end of the text to which the character style is applied.

Figure 17.2
Character codes.

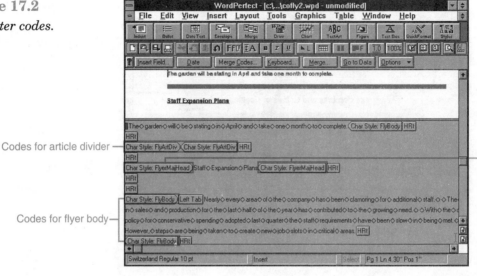

Codes for article divider

Codes for flyer body

Codes for major heading

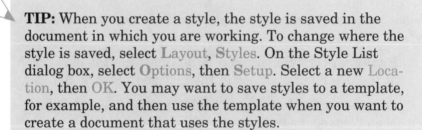

TIP: When you create a style, the style is saved in the document in which you are working. To change where the style is saved, select Layout, Styles. On the Style List dialog box, select Options, then Setup. Select a new Location, then OK. You may want to save styles to a template, for example, and then use the template when you want to create a document that uses the styles.

Creating a Style

To create a style, press Alt + F8, or select Styles from the Layout menu. The Style List dialog box appears. Select Create. The Styles Editor dialog box appears (see Figure 17.3).

In the Style Name text box, type in a name for the style. Type in a Description. Enter a description that distinguishes the style from other styles (such as its use or font type). Select a style Type.

Figure 17.3

The Styles Editor dialog box.

Always use a unique name when you create a
style. Otherwise, you may inadvertently replace an
existing style.

Choose Contents to enter the codes and text that make up the
style. In Figure 17.4, the font and font size are identified. The
center code appears, followed by the standard text to be used every
time the style is used. A hard return is entered.

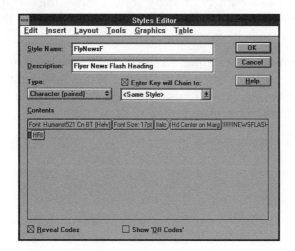

Figure 17.4

Contents entered in the Styles Editor dialog box.

TIP: You can cut or copy codes from your document into Contents. Use F8 or the mouse to select the text. Then, select Edit followed by Cut or Copy. Go into the Contents, and select Edit, Paste to retrieve the cut or copied text.

Still on the Styles Editor dialog box, for Paragraph and Character styles, you can check a check box to Show 'Off Codes'. A code showing where the style ends will be placed in your document.

Normally, when you press Enter, a hard return is placed in your document, and the style is not turned off. You need to remember to move your insertion point past the style's off codes (if entered). If you want to change the action of the Enter key when in a Paragraph or Character Style, check the Enter Key will Chain to check box, and make a selection. These are the options:

<Same Style>: Pressing Enter moves the insertion point past the style then turns the style on again. This is useful for bulleted lists, or when you want to insert text between styles later.

<None>: When you press Enter, your insertion point goes past the style. This option is useful for headings.

(*You can select any existing style.*): Pressing Enter moves the insertion point past the style, and turns on the style you indicate here.

Once you have completed the contents of the style, select OK to leave the Styles Editor dialog box. The style is created, and the style becomes available for use in the Styles List dialog box. Select the Close button to return to your document.

The following Quick Steps summarize how to create a style.

Creating a Style

1. To create a style, press Alt+F8, or select Styles from the Layout menu.

   The Styles List dialog box appears.

2. Select Create.

   The Styles Editor dialog box appears.

3. Complete the Style Name, Description, Type, and Contents. Check any check boxes desired. Select OK.

   The style is added to the Style List dialog box.

4. Select Close.

   You are returned to your document.

TIP: You may create a style of existing formatting. To do this, place your insertion point on the formatted text. Press Alt+F8, or select Styles from the Layout menu. Select Quick Create. Enter a Style Name and Description. Identify the Style Type and select OK.

Using a Style

To use a style, position your insertion point or select text as necessary. Press Alt+F8, or select Styles from the Layout menu. The available styles appear on the Style List dialog box. Highlight the style you want, and choose Apply. The style codes are placed in your document.

Any formatting you enter in your document takes priority over the formatting in the style. That way, if you want to turn off (or add) style attributes for a single occurrence, you can do so. For example, you can have a style that includes a font code and margin codes, but doesn't include underlining of text. You can add the underline code in the document, and use the remaining codes from the style.

The following Quick Steps detail how to use a style.

QUICK STEPS

Using a Style

1. To create a style, press
   Alt + F8 , or select Styles
   from the Layout menu.

   The available styles appear
   on the Style List dialog
   box.

2. Highlight the style you
   want, and choose Apply.

   The style codes are placed
   in your document.

Other Style Options

You may have noticed some other options on the Styles List dialog box. Among these options are ways to edit, copy, delete, save, or retrieve existing styles.

When you select Edit on the Style List dialog box, you are taken to the Styles Editor dialog box, which allows you to change any element of the selected style. The edits affect all occurrences of that style in your current document. (To affect another document, you must make the document active, and then retrieve the new, edited style. A description of this retrieve function appears later in this section.) When you are done editing, the name for the new style appears on the Style List screen. The name of the style you edited is gone.

Copying a style is especially useful if you are creating a template with a variety of styles, and want to add an existing document style to the template. To copy a style, select Options on the Style List dialog box, then Copy. On the Styles Copy dialog box, identify where you want to copy to, and choose OK.

To delete a style for a single section of text, delete the styles code in Reveal Codes. Use the Delete option on the Style List dialog box to delete all occurrences of a style in a document. Just highlight the style you want to delete, and select Options, Delete. The Delete Style dialog box appears. Identify whether you want to delete a style in one of these ways:

Include Codes: Deletes the style and all related codes in your document. Use this option if you want all traces of the style formatting (as well as the style) removed from your document.

Leave Codes: The style is deleted, and the style codes are removed from your document, but the codes that made up the style remain. Use this option if you no longer want to use the style, but don't want to alter the formatting of the document.

The typical way to save styles to be used in different documents is to save them to a template. You can, however, save the styles you create for a document to a file, and then retrieve that style file to use with other documents. This is useful if you have developed some all-purpose styles. To save styles, select Options, Save As from the Style List dialog box. The Save Styles To... dialog box appears. Enter the filename. (Use the .STY extension to easily identify the style file.) Select OK.

You may retrieve a style file (or particular styles) from another document. The styles you retrieve are saved with the document. To retrieve styles to use with an active document, select Options, Retrieve from the Style List dialog box. On the Retrieve Styles From... dialog box, enter the filename, and select OK.

Saving a File to a New Format

1. Press F3 or select Save As from the File menu.
2. Enter the Filename and Format from the list, and then select OK.

Opening or Inserting a File

1. Press Ctrl+O, or select Open from the File menu (or use File from the Insert menu).
2. Identify the file you want to open or insert, specify the type, and choose OK.

Importing Spreadsheet or Database Information

1. Place the insertion point where the data will be placed.
2. Select Spreadsheet/Database from the Insert menu. Select Import.
3. Enter the options, and then select OK.

Linking Spreadsheet or Database Information

1. Place the insertion point where the data will be placed.
2. Select Spreadsheet/Database from the Insert menu. Select Create Link.
3. Enter the options, and then select OK.

Getting Information From and To Other Sources

This chapter covers several methods of transferring information into and out of WordPerfect for Windows from other sources. For example, you can bring spreadsheet information developed with another program into a WordPerfect document. Or you can save your WordPerfect document into a format that can be used by another program. This is handy if you need to share a WordPerfect file with someone who uses another word processor, or if you need to send information over the phone lines via a modem.

Saving to Another Format

To save a WordPerfect document to another format, make the window containing the document active. Press F3, or select Save As from the File menu. Enter the name you want to give the exported version, including the proper extension for the format into which you're exporting. (For example, MS Word uses .DOC for its files, so if you are exporting in MS Word format, you might want to call your file NEWFILE.DOC.)

Once the name of the file is entered, select Format. A drop-down list (shown in Figure 18.1) appears. This list shows the formats in which a WordPerfect document can be saved. The default selection is **WordPerfect 6.0**. However, the list includes formats for other versions of WordPerfect, and for other popular word processing programs. You may also choose all-purpose formats including ANSI, ASCII Text, Navy DIF Standard, and Rich Text Format (RTF).

Figure 18.1

Save As dialog box with format options.

Saving Plain Text

Plain formats like ASCII Text export the file without its formatting (such as margins and italics). Why would you want to export into a format like that? Here's an example. Let's say you're using an electronic publishing program, and find that the specific file format for that program is not listed. In this case, you could save the WordPerfect file in the ASCII format (sometimes known as the *DOS text format*). Then, import the ASCII file into your electronic publishing package. Some format settings may be lost, but the retyping time saved is usually well worth any changes that need to be made.

Once you have selected the file format, select OK. The new file is created.

TIP: Always save the document in WordPerfect format too, so you'll have the document to refer to later. Use the regular File Save command.

Opening or Inserting Documents from Other Programs

Users of WordPerfect version 6.0 for Windows will be happy to learn that files from other versions of WordPerfect can be exchanged. When you retrieve a document created in WordPerfect 5.1 or 6.0 for DOS, or WordPerfect 5.1 or 5.2 for Windows, no intervention is needed on your part. WordPerfect converts the file, and your formatting is maintained.

WordPerfect is set up to allow you to open files from popular brand-name word processors (such as MS Word and Ami Pro) in their own file formats. It also handles industry-standard personal computer formats common to word processing, spreadsheet, and database programs; these include Spreadsheet DIF, Rich Text Format (RTF), and ASCII.

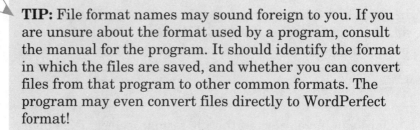

TIP: File format names may sound foreign to you. If you are unsure about the format used by a program, consult the manual for the program. It should identify the format in which the files are saved, and whether you can convert files from that program to other common formats. The program may even convert files directly to WordPerfect format!

If you open a file that was created in another format, a **Convert File Format** message box appears. Select OK and WordPerfect for Windows will convert the file. If WordPerfect can't convert the file, a message lets you know. The best way to go is to save the file in the original program to a common file format (like ASCII), and then open the document in WordPerfect. The manual for the other program should tell you how to save in ASCII format.

To import a document created by another program, press Ctrl+O, or select Open from the File menu. Or use File from the Insert menu to insert the file's contents where your insertion point rests. Depending on your choice, the Open File or Insert File dialog box appears. Select (or type the filename of) the file you want to open or insert. To ensure that the format type is as close to that of your file as possible, check the List Files of Type drop-down box. Figure 18.2 illustrates the Open File dialog box, with WP Merge Data selected. Choose a new format from the drop-down list, if appropriate. Once the correct type of file to convert from appears, select OK. The file is converted and appears.

Once the file is opened, make any edits you like, then use File, Save As to save the document to WordPerfect 6.0 format.

TIP: You may want to use a spreadsheet or database file as a WordPerfect merged data file. For example, you may have a client list created through a database program, which you want to use in creating merged, personalized letters. To retrieve a spreadsheet or database file as a merged data file, use the WP Merge Data type of file. This type adds *delimiters* (which are characters that identify the start and end of each field and of each record).

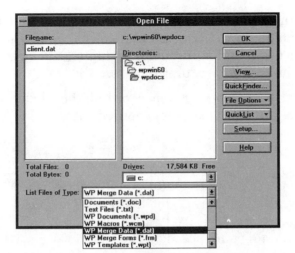

Figure 18.2
Open File dialog box with WP Merge Data selected.

TIP: When shipping text from a file created by one program to WordPerfect (and vice versa), Windows users enjoy a special shortcut. Select the text to place in the new file, then cut or copy the text to the Clipboard. Go to the new file and position the insertion point. Paste the contents of the Clipboard to the new location.

Working with Spreadsheets and Databases

In addition to the alternatives covered thus far, there are some special methods for bringing spreadsheet and database data into existing WordPerfect documents. Two Spreadsheet\Database alternatives are available: *importing* and *linking*.

- Importing data is useful for including the data in memos, reports, and letters that will be generated once.

- Linking data means the information can be updated automatically in both files when a change is made in one. Links are useful for documents that change over time, such as lists and regular reports.

In both cases, you can import or link the whole spreadsheet or database, or just a *range* (portion) of data.

CAUTION   The Import and Link features were designed to work with the most popular spreadsheets and databases on the market, including most versions of Lotus 1-2-3, Excel, and Quattro Pro. Check with WordPerfect Corporation if your spreadsheet or database data does not seem to be importing or linking as described. You may have a spreadsheet or database that is not supported by this feature.

Importing Spreadsheet or Database Data

Importing spreadsheet or database data brings the data into the file exactly as it is at the moment. If you make changes to the data in the future using your spreadsheet or database program, the WordPerfect document will not be affected.

You can import an entire spreadsheet or database or a part of one (using the Range option), and you can import it either as text (with tabs), in a WordPerfect table, or as a merged data file. To import, use the following Quick Steps.

Importing a Spreadsheet or Database

1. Place the insertion point where the data will be imported.

   The insertion point identifies the position for importing the data.

2. Select Spreadsheet/ Database from the Insert menu. Select Import.

   The Import Data dialog box appears (Figure 18.3).

3. Make the necessary selections to enter the Data Type, Import As, the Filename, and the Range of the file to import. Then select OK.

   The spreadsheet or database is imported.

Figure 18.3
The Import Data dialog box.

Select Import when the settings are all made. The spreadsheet or database data is imported. Figure 18.4 shows a spreadsheet imported into a document. Notice that the spreadsheet (imported as text rather than a table) has tabs inserted.

Figure 18.4
*The result of
importing a
spreadsheet.*

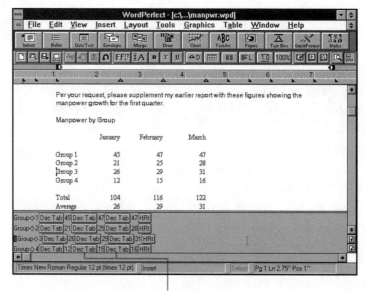

Tabs take the place of cell gridlines.

Linking Spreadsheet or Database Data

When you import data, the information in your WordPerfect document is not updated when you update the spreadsheet or database. If you *link* the spreadsheet or database data, however, the linked document can be updated when you update the spreadsheet or database.

The procedure for linking is very similar to that of importing. Follow these Quick Steps to link a spreadsheet or database file.

Linking a Spreadsheet or Database

1. Place the insertion point where the data will be placed.

   The insertion point identifies the position for the data.

2. Select Spreadsheet/ Database from the Insert menu. Select Create Link.

   The Create Data Link dialog box appears (Figure 18.5).

3. Enter the options you want for Data Type, Link As, Filename, and Range; then select OK.

   The data is linked.

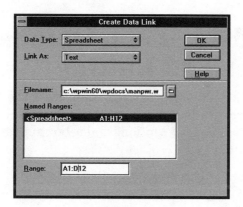

Figure 18.5
The Create Data Link dialog box.

An example of a completed link is shown in Figure 18.6. The beginning of the link is displayed on the screen as an icon. The information includes the path and filename. A code beginning with **[Link]** appears in Reveal Codes. At the end of the link, another icon is placed in your document, and a **[Link]** code is shown in Reveal Codes.

Figure 18.6
Result of link.

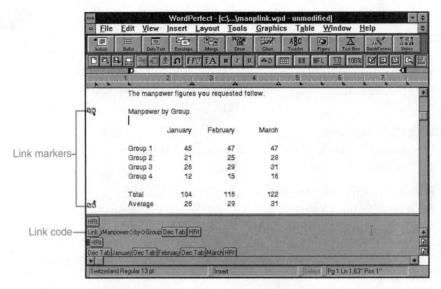

Link markers─

Link code─

Spreadsheet and Database Options and Editing

If you don't like the on-screen icon display of the link beginning and end, select Spreadsheet/Database from the Insert menu. Select Options. The Link Options dialog box appears. Deselect the check box Show Link Icons.

The Link Options dialog box also has a check box for Update on Retrieve. Check this check box if you want WordPerfect for Windows to update the data automatically when the WordPerfect document is retrieved. If you leave the check box blank, you can update the spreadsheet or database information manually. To update manually, select Spreadsheet/Database from the Insert menu then Update. On the Update dialog box, respond Yes to update all data links.

If you want to delete the link (but not the spreadsheet or database information), delete either the beginning or ending code in Reveal Codes.

To edit a single link, place your insertion point between the beginning and ending link codes. Select Spreadsheet/Database from the Insert menu, then Edit Link. The Edit Data Link dialog box appears. You can change the Data Type, Link As, Filename, or Range. Then select OK.

TIP: If you import or link large spreadsheets or databases, you may run into space problems. If the row is too long, the data displayed as text will wrap around on the line, and the data in table format will be cut off. Either condition may give you an undesirable outcome. Possible solutions include:

- Reduce the column width in the spreadsheet or database program (if the columns can be made smaller without losing the contents). For instructions on how to resize, reduce, or change the width of columns, see the documentation for the spreadsheet or database program.

- Change the base font affecting the imported spreadsheet information in WordPerfect. Select Font from the Layout menu. Select a small font.

- Change the margins in WordPerfect by selecting Margins from the Layout menu.

- Change the orientation of the paper to landscape by selecting Page from the Layout menu. Select Paper Size.

- If the spreadsheet or database is imported as a table, size the table to fit between the margins. Select Tables.

Read about these options (and hints for handling more complicated import and export tasks) in an advanced WordPerfect for Windows text.

Inserting Graphics

You may use the Graphics menu (see Chapter 16) to place graphics in a WordPerfect document. WordPerfect supports the graphic files created by most programs; the file extensions of their formats include CGM, DXF (AutoCAD), EPS, GEM, PCX, PIC (Lotus), TIFF, and more. Alternatively, you may launch the software for the graphic from within WordPerfect, select or create an object, and insert it into the WordPerfect document at your insertion point.

To insert an object:

1. Select Insert then Object. The Insert Object dialog box appears.

2. Identify the Object type from those that appear, and select OK. Remember, the program for the type of object you select must be available to be started automatically by WordPerfect. The program is launched.

3. Create a graphic, or select an existing graphic.

4. Exit the program and return to your document. Typically, an option like "Exit & Return to Document1" appears on the File menu.

5. When a message like that shown in Figure 18.7 appears, select Yes. Do not close the connection between the open embedded object and your WordPerfect document. Instead, update the embedded document.

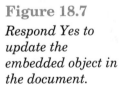

Figure 18.7

Respond Yes to update the embedded object in the document.

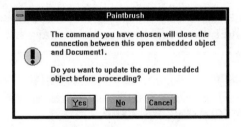

Creating a Table of Contents and Index

1. Mark each entry.
2. Define the Table of Contents and Index.
3. Generate the Table of Contents and Index.

Marking a Table of Contents Entry

1. Select Table of Contents from the Tools menu.
2. Select the entry, then the appropriate Mark button.

Marking an Index Entry

1. Select Index from the Tools menu.
2. Complete the Heading and Subheading entries as desired, by selecting or typing in text.
3. Select Mark.

Defining a Table of Contents or Index

1. Place your insertion point where the table of contents or index should appear.
2. From the Table of Contents or Index Feature Bar, select Define. Complete the related define dialog box, and choose OK.

Generating a Table of Contents and Index

1. From either the Table of Contents or Index Feature Bar, select Generate.
2. Choose OK to confirm.

19

Tables of Contents and Indexes

WordPerfect for Windows has a wealth of organizational features to make your job easier. Among them is the capability of generating tables of contents, indexes, and outlines automatically. This chapter details how it works.

The old-fashioned way of creating a table of contents or an index is to identify the text manually in your document (after all page numbers have been assigned), and then type in each entry, along with the page number. If the document is edited and the page numbers change, the table of contents and index have to be updated manually.

With WordPerfect for Windows, however, the process of creating tables of contents and indexes is greatly simplified. In the document, you mark the text that is to be included in the table of contents or index. Then when you give the signal, WordPerfect for Windows generates the table of contents or index automatically. When the document is edited, just ask WordPerfect to generate the references again. There's no manual record-keeping of what's in the index and table of contents, no manual updating, and no chance of a page-numbering error.

Creating a Table of Contents or Index

To create a table of contents or index, follow these basic steps:

1. Mark the text you want to include in the table of contents or index. This identifies the entries to WordPerfect.

2. Define the characteristics of the table of contents or index. You can identify the location and appearance of a table of contents, and the location for index words.

3. Generate the table of contents or index. WordPerfect finds each occurrence of the text marked for a table of contents or an index, and creates the references.

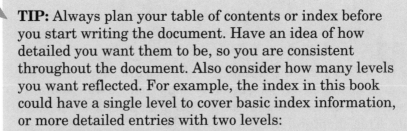

TIP: Always plan your table of contents or index before you start writing the document. Have an idea of how detailed you want them to be, so you are consistent throughout the document. Also consider how many levels you want reflected. For example, the index in this book could have a single level to cover basic index information, or more detailed entries with two levels:

index
    generating
    marking and defining

The procedures for *marking* and *defining* tables of contents and indexes are slightly different, so we'll discuss them separately in the following sections. (The procedure for *generating* them is the same; you'll learn how near the end of the chapter.)

Marking and Defining a Table of Contents

You can create a table of contents with one to five levels. Each additional level is a *sublevel*. Figure 19.1 shows part of a table of contents for a document created by Barbara J. Wiley. It has only one level. Figure 19.2 shows a portion of Wiley's table of contents, this time with two levels. Each new sublevel in a table of contents is indented to the next tab stop.

Developing a Computer System
By Barbara J. Wiley and Paul G. Otto

Table of Contents

Major Tasks 1
Specification 7
Design 13
Coding 19
Implementation 26
Post Implementation 14

Figure 19.1
Table of contents with one level.

Developing a Computer System
By Barbara J. Wiley and Paul G. Otto

Table of Contents

Major Tasks 1
    Specification 2
    Design 3
    Coding 3
    Implementation 5
    Post Implementation 6
Specification 7
    The Goal 8
    User Requirements 8
    The Role of MIS 10
Design 13
    The Goal 13
    The Team 15
    The Detail System Design Document 18
Coding 19
Implementation 26
Post Implementation 14

Figure 19.2
Table of contents with two levels.

The first step in creating a table of contents or index is marking each item in the document that needs to be included. The following Quick Steps show how to mark an entry for a table of contents.

Quick Steps

Marking a Table of Contents Entry

1. Select Table of Contents from the Tools menu.

   The Table of Contents Feature Bar (shown in Figure 19.3) appears.

2. Select the entry with F8, or use the mouse.

   The entry for the table of contents is identified.

3. Mark the text at the level number you want (1, 2, 3, 4, or 5) by selecting the appropriate Mark button.

   Codes are placed around the text. For example, these codes show that the word **Coding** is a level 1 table of contents entry:

   [Mrk Txt ToC:1]
   Coding**[Mrk Txt ToC: 1]**

Figure 19.3

The Table of Contents Feature Bar.

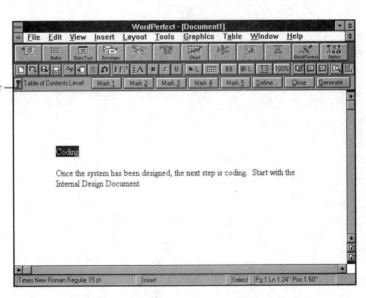

Once all of the table of contents entries are marked, you must define the table of contents. Use these Quick Steps:

Defining a Table of Contents

1. Place your insertion point where you want the table of contents to appear. Typically, you will want it at the beginning of the document on its own page. To create a page, enter a hard page break with `Ctrl`+`↵Enter`. You can also enter a heading, such as **Contents**.

   The starting location for the table of contents is established.

2. Select Table of Contents from the Tools menu, then Define from the Table of Contents Feature Bar.

   The Define Table of Contents dialog box appears.

3. Identify the number of levels by selecting Number of Levels and typing in a number 1 through 5.

4. Select a Numbering Format to choose how page numbers are to be displayed.

   Table 19.1 shows the choices with examples.

5. If you want to select a style to use, select Styles, and complete the options on the Table of Contents Styles dialog box. Select OK. (See Chapter 17 for information on styles.)

   You are returned to the Define Table of Contents dialog box.

continues

continued

6. To enter a page number format, select Page Numbering, and complete the dialog box. Select OK. (See Chapter 9 for information on page numbering.)

You return to the Define Table of Contents dialog box.

7. Leave the check box Display Last Level in Wrapped Format unchecked.

This prevents the levels from wrapping around as if they were part of one paragraph.

8. Select OK when you are done.

On screen, this message appears: **<< Table of Contents will generate here >>**. A code like this appears in your document: **[Def Mark: TofC,3:Dot Ldr #]**.

Table 19.1
Numbering Format Choices

Format	Appearance
No Numbering (no page numbers)	**Major Tasks**
Text # (page number follows entry)	**Major Tasks 1**
Text (#) (page number in parenthesis follows entry)	**Major Tasks (1)**
Text # (page number flush right)	**Major Tasks** 1
Text......# (page number flush right with dot leaders)	**Major Tasks** 1

The code starts with the *Definition mark* for the table of contents. There are three levels, and the page numbering on each level will have dot leaders.

Once you have marked the table of contents entries and defined the table of contents, you can generate it—which is discussed in "Generating the Table of Contents and Index," later in this chapter. Because you generate both the table of contents and index at the same time, you may want to mark and define an index first.

Marking and Defining an Index

When you create an index, you can use headings and subheadings, as shown in Figure 19.4. Notice that the subheadings are indented under the associated heading. The tab stops are used for indentation. In Figure 19.4, the heading is **Coding** and the subheading is **Common Problems and Solutions**.

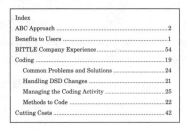

Figure 19.4

Index with headings and subheadings.

The following Quick Steps summarize the process of marking an index entry.

Marking an Index Entry

1. Select Index from the Tools menu.

   The Index Feature Bar appears.

2. Select the text for the heading, and select the Heading button or type in text.

   The heading appears.

3. Enter the subheading (if any).

   The subheading appears.

4. Choose Mark.

   Codes are placed in your document. The following code indicates the word **Shoes** is an index entry: **[Index:Shoes]**.

There is one other method you can use in identifying words for an index. You can create a *concordance file*, which is a list of words you want in the index. WordPerfect for Windows looks for and marks these words in your document. You can check each mark, adding and deleting marks as you want. For more information on using a concordance file, see your WordPerfect Reference.

Once all index entries are marked, define the index. To do this, follow these Quick Steps:

Defining the Index

1. Place your insertion point where you want the index to appear in your document.

   The starting point for the index is established.

2. Select Index from the Tools menu then Define from the Index Feature Bar.

   The Define Index dialog box appears (see Figure 19.5).

3. Select any numbering format options desired.

4. Select Change to change the current style of the index, if desired. Select OK.

A code like this is placed in your document: **[Def Mark:Index,Dot Ldr #]**. This identifies where the index will be placed, and the type of page numbering it will use.

NOTE: The Numbering Format options allow you to identify the Position of the page number and the Page Numbering format. These options are the same as those for defining a table of contents. If you want a dash to separate consecutive pages, check Use Dash to Show Consecutive Pages.

The following text appears on your screen until the index is generated: **<< Index will generate here >>**.

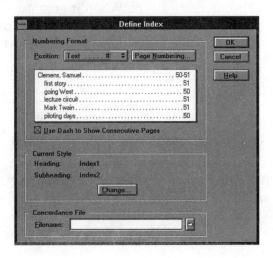

Figure 19.5

Define Index dialog box appears.

Generating the Table of Contents and Index

The procedure is the same for generating a table of contents as for an index. In fact, if you have marked entries for both, you will generate both when you follow these Quick Steps:

QUICK
STEPS

Generating a TOC or Index

1. Select either Table of Contents or Index from the Tools menu.

   The Feature Bar for the chosen option appears.

2. Select Generate.

   The Generate dialog box appears with this message: **Generate Table of Contents, Table of Authorities, Indexes, Cross-References and Lists.**

3. Select OK.

   A message appears as the generation is completed. When it goes away, the table of contents and index have been generated, and appear.

CAUTION

Never delete the **[Def Mark]** codes. If you do, WordPerfect for Windows will not know where to put the table of contents or index if you generate it again. The only time to delete these codes is if you are deleting the entire table of contents or index.

Once the table of contents or index has been generated, you can edit it like any document. For example, you can add your own headings and blank lines, or change tab settings to alter the indentation.

The page numbers in the table of contents and index remain the same until you generate them again. As a result, when you edit a document, the page numbers in the table of contents and index do not change automatically. When you are done making changes in the document, select Generate from the appropriate Feature Bar, and proceed. (Alternatively, you may select Generate from the Tools menu, or press Ctrl+F9.)

TIP: Usually you will want to generate your table of contents and index after spell checking, but before printing your document. This way, all editing will be complete, and the page numbers will be stable. Sometimes, however, it is useful to generate the table of contents or index as you work. Doing so provides a reference that lets you see the structure of the document, and the location of particular material. You can generate a table of contents and index again and again.

Creative Uses of Tables of Contents and Indexes

Don't let names fool you. You can use the Table of Contents and Index functions for applications other than generating these specialized documents. The Table of Contents feature can be used to create any list of items that follows the order they appear in the document. The Index feature places items in alphabetical order, and can be used to associate subordinate items to a superior item. Consider using these functions to put together almost any kind of list.

continues

continued

For example, one clever user composed a narrative of her family, and used the Index feature of WordPerfect to generate a family tree automatically. (Children were marked as subordinate items to parents.) Open your mind. Use the Table of Contents and Index features to create vocabulary lists, short narrative summaries, lists of figures or graphics, or any form of list.

Creating Outlines

Outlining is another useful organizing technique WordPerfect for Windows makes easy. You can switch to the Outline mode, and the text you type will be numbered and indented automatically; you don't have to remember what number or letter comes next, or how far to indent. Also, numbers and letters are updated automatically when you edit the outline. Figure 19.6 illustrates part of an outline created using WordPerfect.

Figure 19.6

An outline created with WordPerfect for Windows.

```
Talk for Data Processing Professional Group
By Barbara J. Wiley
I.    Background of presenters
II.   Why computer systems haven't met needs
III.  Benefits of a better approach
IV.   Major Tasks
      A.  Specifications
          1.  The stated and hidden goals
          2.  Getting user requirements
          3.  Story of BITTLE
          4.  MIS role (new and old)
      B.  Design
```

To develop an outline, first follow these Quick Steps to begin using the Outline feature.

Beginning a New Outline

1. Place the insertion point where the outline will start.

2. Select Outline from the Tools menu.

   The Outline Feature Bar appears.

3. To change the numbering style, select Options, then Define Outline. Select any Name you want (such as bullets, Numbers, etc.).

   The Description of the Name appears.

4. Select OK.

   You return to your document.

Text you enter will be in outline form. Certain keypresses give results in Outline mode that differ from those in regular editing mode.

Type in text (to go to the next level, press Tab⇥), or click on the right arrow button on the Outline Feature Bar. To go back a level, press ⇧Shift+Tab⇥, or click on the left arrow button on the Feature Bar. Continue using these keys while you create your outline. Table 19.2 summarizes the keys to press, buttons to click on, and the results.

Key to press	Click on	Result
Tab⇥	Right arrow button	To go in (right) one level
⇧Shift+Tab⇥	Left arrow button	To go out (left) one level

Table 19.2
Presses or Clicks While Outlining

When you insert a level number, a code for paragraph style appears in the text:

[Para Style:Level 1]

For example, to re-create the outline in Figure 19.6, follow these steps:

1. After the outline title and Barbara J. Wiley's byline, begin an outline (as shown in the previous Quick Steps). Select Outline from the Tools menu.

2. Select Options, Define Outline. Choose Outline and select OK. The first line will be numbered **I** automatically.

3. Type in the text. Press ⏎Enter at the end of the line. A **II** appears. Type in the next line, doing the same for lines **III** and **IV**. Press ⏎Enter at the end of each line.

4. To go to a new level, press Tab⇥. The number **V** disappears, and is replaced with the letter **A**.

5. Type Specification, press ⏎Enter and Tab⇥ to go to a new level, the number **1**.

6. From the line marked 1 through the line marked 4, type in a line, and press ⏎Enter at the end of each line.

7. After line 4, **5** appears. Press ⇧Shift+Tab⇥ to move left one tab setting. The **5** is replaced with the letter **B**.

TIP: Outlining can feel a little cumbersome at first. Most people new to creating outlines take a few minutes to experiment with the keypresses to get the hang of the actions. Once you become familiar with the results, you'll pick up speed.

When you are done creating the outline, select Options from the Feature Bar, and End Outline. You are returned to regular editing mode. A code is placed in the document.

This description of outlining will get you started. If you use outlining often and want to learn a few tricks, consult your WordPerfect Reference. For example, there are keypresses that move you more than one level at a time, and to the most recent occurrence of the same level.

Displaying the Button Bar

- To see or hide a Button Bar, select Button Bar from the View menu.

Choosing a Button Bar

1. From the File menu, select Preferences, then the Button Bar icon. Or click the right mouse button on the Button Bar, and select Preferences.

2. Highlight a Button Bar, and choose Select.

Creating and Editing a Button Bar

1. From the File menu, select Preferences, then the Button Bar icon. Or click the right mouse button on the Button Bar, and select Preferences.

2. Choose Create, enter a name, and select OK. Or highlight the Button Bar you want to edit, and select Edit.

3. You can add, delete, move, and customize buttons. Select OK when done.

20

Button Bars and the Power Bar

Button Bars can be used to perform any operation you want—whether it is a command, a series of commands, or a macro—with a quick click of the mouse. Because you set up the operation, you control what the Button Bar performs. You can use one of WordPerfect for Windows' supplied Button Bars, or you can create any number of Button Bars and edit them at any time.

You may edit the Power Bar according to a set of options more limited than those for a Button Bar. For example, you cannot attach macros or commands to a button in the Power Bar.

TIP: When to use a Button Bar versus the Power Bar? Among the functions available from the Power Bar, select those you use most for your customized Power Bar. Place other options, macros, and keystroke commands on the Button Bar. If you use operations regularly that are not on the Power Bar, they are good candidates for the Button Bar. If you have a macro you use often, put it on a Button Bar. For example, you may have several macros that

continues

continued

create documents with common formatting, and fill-ins for (perhaps) a memo, letter, standard report, or status report. If you set up a macro to open each document, and then assign these macros to a Button Bar, you can get to any of these frequently-used documents quickly.

Displaying and Using a Button Bar

To see a Button Bar, select Button Bar from the View menu. The Button Bar command is marked, and the current Button Bar will display until you change the selection (even if you leave and return to WordPerfect for Windows).

WordPerfect comes with a several general-use Button Bars already set up for you. The Button Bar shown in Figure 20.1 may appear when you first select Button Bar from the View menu. To see what each button on the bar does, place your mouse pointer over a button. The button's use appears at the top of the screen.

Figure 20.1
WordPerfect's Button Bar and Power Bar.

Button Bar ——

Power Bar ——

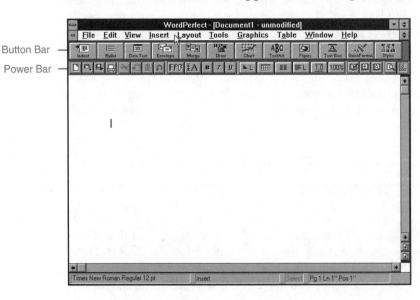

To hide the Button Bar, just uncheck the option by selecting Button Bar from the View menu. Or click the right mouse button on the Button Bar. A QuickMenu appears. Choose Hide Button Bar.

Changing the Button Bar

To change the Button Bar that appears when you select Button Bar from the View menu, select Preferences from the File menu. Select the Button Bar icon. The Button Bar Preferences dialog box appears (see Figure 20.2). To see what buttons appear on a particular bar, select it from the list. The buttons appear on your screen.

Figure 20.2
The Button Bar Preferences dialog box.

To choose a new default Button Bar, highlight your choice among Available Button Bars and choose Select. A shortcut to choosing a new Button Bar is to click the right mouse button on the current Button Bar. Choose a new Button Bar from the QuickMenu.

Moving the Button Bar

The Button Bar can be moved to a new spot on the document window. Place the mouse pointer on a space between buttons on the bar (the pointer will look like a hand). Drag the Button Bar to the new location. Later in this chapter, you'll learn how to enter a setting to affect the location of Button Bars.

Creating and Editing a Button Bar

Once you get used to the quickness of the Button Bar, you will want to customize your own. For example, if you use many macros, you may want a Button Bar just for your macros. You may also want to edit existing Button Bars. The steps for creating and editing Button Bars are similar.

To create or edit a Button Bar, select Preferences, then **Button Bar** from the File menu. Or click the right mouse button on the Button Bar itself, and select Preferences from the QuickMenu that appears. Then the Button Bar Preferences dialog box appears. To edit a Button Bar, highlight the Button Bar first, then choose Edit. You are taken to the Button Bar Editor, shown in Figure 20.3.

To create a Button Bar, also start from the Button Bar Preferences dialog box. Choose Create. On the Create Button Bar dialog box, give the Button Bar a name. If you want to change the template the Button Bar is stored with, select Template, complete the option, and select OK. Once the information on the Create Button Bar dialog box is complete, select OK. You are taken to the Button Bar Editor (see Figure 20.3).

Figure 20.3
*The Button Bar
Editor.*

You can use the Edit Button Bar dialog box to perform several types of additions to the Button Bar. Select one of the following "Add a Button To" options:

Activate a Feature: Choose this option to select from long lists of WordPerfect features. First, choose from the Feature/Categories. Then, select a Feature. Select Add Button when the selection is complete. The button appears.

Play a Keyboard Script: Select this option, then type in the keystrokes the command should play. Select Add Script and the button is added. Approximately the first ten characters in the keystrokes are used as the name of the button. (We'll cover how to change button names later on.)

Launch a Program: Choose this option to run a program. Choose Select File to choose the execution file for the program (usually execution files end in EXE). Select OK. The button appears with the name of the file.

Play a Macro: Use this option to select an existing macro to be run when the button is selected. Choose Add Macro. Identify the name of the macro, and choose Select. The button is given the same name as the macro.

Continue to use the Button Bar Editor to add buttons. To delete a button, simply drag it from the Button Bar. To move a button, drag it to the new location. To enter a space, drag the Separator< icon to the location. To customize a button, double-click on it. The Customize a Button dialog box appears. You may change the text on the button, the description that appears when the mouse passes over the button, or the graphic for the button. Select OK on the Button Bar Editor when you are done, then Close.

> **CAUTION**
>
> As you build the Button Bar, don't select the same option twice. Although WordPerfect for Windows will let you do it, it is a waste of good button space.

Once the Button Bar is created, you may select it for use. Figure 20.4 illustrates the completed Button Bar, including a button for the BRETADD macro (the example from Chapter 14) set off by spaces.

TIP: If you add more buttons than can appear on a Button Bar, the bar extends off the screen. Later, when you want to access buttons that are off the screen, you can click on the arrows in the Button Bar to move the bar and expose the button you want. See the arrows in Figure 20.4.

Figure 20.4
The complete Button Bar.

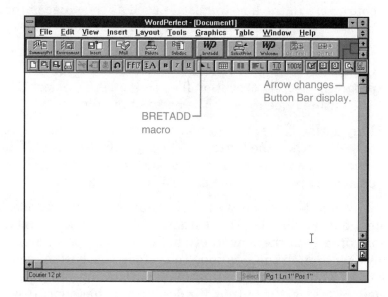

The following Quick Steps summarize how to create or edit a Button Bar.

Creating or Editing a Button Bar

1. From the File menu, select Preferences, then Button Bar (or click the right mouse button on the Button Bar itself, and select Preferences).

2. Choose Create, name the new Button Bar, and select OK. Or highlight the Button Bar you want to edit, and select Edit.	The Button Bar Editor dialog box appears.
3. Add, delete, move, and customize buttons as you want. Select OK when you are done.	The Button Bar is available for use.

Manipulating the Button Bar

You can manipulate an entire Button Bar at once. Use the Button Bar Preferences dialog box (accessed via Preferences on the QuickMenu or File, Preferences, Button Bar).

For example, the font and size of the Button Bar can be changed. From the Button Bar Preferences dialog box, select Options. You may change the Font Face or Font Size. You may also affect the Appearance. The options are Text only, Picture only, or Picture and Text. Finally, the Location can be changed. The options are Left, Top, Right, Bottom, Palette.

Figure 20.5 shows the Button Bar Options dialog box, with **System Fonts** selected as the Font Face. Notice that the buttons are increased in size to accommodate the font face.

The Button Bar Preferences dialog box can also be used to delete a Button Bar. Just highlight the bar on the list that you want to delete, and select Delete. You will receive a confirmation message. Select Yes.

Finally, you may use the Button Bar Preferences dialog box to copy a Button Bar. Select Copy. Use the lists to identify the template to copy from, the Button Bars to copy, and the template to copy to. Select Copy.

Figure 20.5

The system font is selected in the Button Bar Options dialog box, and shown in the Button Bar displayed above it.

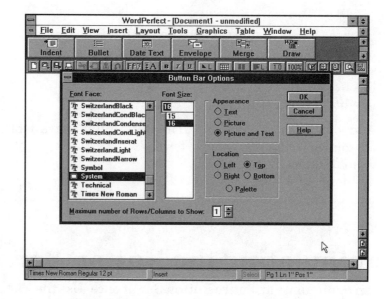

The Power Bar

You may use the default Power Bar that comes with WordPerfect for Windows, or you may change it and return later to the default Power Bar. You cannot "store" multiple Power Bars as you can Button Bars, however. Nor may you assign macros or keystrokes to a Power Bar.

Controlling the Power Bar

To display the Power Bar, select Power Bar from the View menu. To hide the Power Bar, deselect it on the View menu, or place the mouse pointer on the Power Bar and press the right mouse button. From the QuickMenu, select Hide Power Bar.

To change the Power Bar, select Preferences, then Power Bar from the File menu. Alternatively, click the right mouse button on the Power Bar, and select Preferences. The Power Bar Preferences dialog box appears. The Items checked are those that appear in the Power Bar. To add an item, check the box. To remove an item, drag it off the Power Bar. To move an item, just drag it to the new location. To add a space, drag the Separator icon to the desired location. Finally, you may select Fonts to identify which True Type font styles will be available when you select the **Font** item on the Power Bar. This way, you can make only those fonts that work with your printer available.

To return to the default Power Bar at any time, you may select Default from the Power Bar Preferences dialog box.

The Basics for Beginners

You may want to fire up your computer and begin punching keys right now. If you spend just a few moments picking up some basic concepts, however, you'll avoid confusion later. Once you have the big picture, you can fill in the details. This appendix will help you understand:

- Word processing
- The parts of your computer
- Keyboard and mouse operation

What Is Word Processing?

Word processing is the term used to describe the development of letters, reports, and other documents with a computer. Word processing offers many advantages over handwriting or typing documents. Speed is a primary advantage. Because most people write by hand at about twelve words per minute, you don't have to be a speed demon on a keyboard to improve your efficiency with word processing. Another advantage you gain with word processing is the greater ease of entering, editing, and printing your work.

You replace the cumbersome cut-paste-and-retype approach with copying, moving, and deleting words instantly. A final, printed copy is only a few keystrokes away. The printed copy is clean, free of erasures and correction fluid.

WordPerfect for Windows is one brand of word processor. WordPerfect has been a best-seller for years because of its simplicity and power. At first, you'll probably create small, straightforward documents. But once you get up and running, and want to go on to more sophisticated word processing, WordPerfect won't hold you back.

The written works you create using WordPerfect are called *documents*. A document can be any written item you create, such as a letter, a report, a memo, an expense sheet, a bill, or a list (to name just a few). You can combine elements in one document (such as following a letter with a bill). You decide how many documents you want to create, and the contents of each document.

A Look at Your Computer

Your computer system includes hardware and software. *Hardware*, the physical part, is made up of the computer parts you can see and touch, while *software* consists of the operating system, and the programs you run—the logical part.

Software Components

Software refers to a computer program stored on a disk. Different programs have different functions. The software that enables the WordPerfect program to interact with your computer hardware is called the *operating system*. On an IBM-compatible PC, your operating system is DOS, which stands for Disk Operating System. The WordPerfect program is another kind of software: an *application*. While the operating system simply keeps the computer up and running, application software helps you perform a task, such as word processing.

Many files make up the WordPerfect for Windows application, each one carrying a specific set of instructions to the computer. There are many different types of files, and each file has a unique, descriptive name. Each WordPerfect document that you create can be stored individually on disk, too, with its own unique name.

Hardware Components

Your computer is made up of many hardware components, which work together to provide a fully functional unit. Figure A.1 illustrates some common hardware components:

Keyboard: The component that resembles the keys on a typewriter, with a few added. You'll enter commands and type documents by pressing keys on the keyboard.

Monitor: The component that looks like a television screen. The text you type appears here, as well as special messages from WordPerfect that prompt you to press certain keys.

Central Processing Unit (CPU): The CPU is the "brains" of the computer, where all the processing takes place. As you work, the WordPerfect program and the documents you type are stored in *random-access memory* (*RAM*). RAM is temporary; its content is cleared when the computer is turned off. That's why it is so important to save your work to a disk.

Hard Disks, Floppy Disks, and Disk Drives: When you save your work, it is transferred from RAM to a disk for permanent storage. Once your work is saved on a disk, you can turn off your computer and retrieve the document from the disk when you use WordPerfect again. The disk may be a *hard disk* (fixed in the computer's case) or a removable 5 1/4-inch or 3 1/2-inch *floppy* (flexible) disk.

Printer (optional): You can use WordPerfect without a printer, but if you do, you can only view your documents on the monitor. You cannot get a *hard copy* of your work without a printer.

Mouse: You can use a mouse to point to and select WordPerfect options, as a substitute for making selections from the keyboard. You will still use the keyboard for typing text, however, and for some WordPerfect functions. Many WordPerfect users prefer a mouse because it seems to be easier and faster to use than the keyboard.

Figure A.1
Computer components.

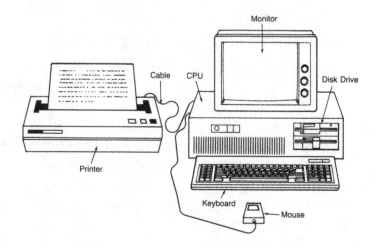

Communicating with Your Computer

There are two ways to issue commands to your computer: with the keyboard and with the mouse. In WordPerfect for Windows, you'll likely want to use a combination of both. The following explains a bit about the keyboard and the mouse in WordPerfect for Windows.

Using Your Keyboard

The computer keyboard lets you communicate with WordPerfect for Windows. The keys on the keyboard are shown in Figure A.2. Many keyboard keys are the same as those on a typewriter; others are special-use keys that access powerful features or shortcuts.

Figure A.2
A typical keyboard.

The following is a description of each group of keys found on the keyboard. Find these on your own keyboard.

- The *Letter / Number / Symbol keys* are common to computers and typewriters. Press these to type letters, numbers, and symbols. Press ⇧Shift to type capital letters, symbols, or punctuation marks found on the top half of these keys.

- The *Function keys* are labeled F1 through F10 (F12 on some computers). They are used to perform special WordPerfect functions. They may be used alone or in conjunction with other keys including Alt, Ctrl, or ⇧Shift. This book uses illustrations of keys, and places a plus (**+**) between two key names, such as ⇧Shift+F1, to indicate you are to press the two keys simultaneously.

- The *cursor arrow keys* (↑ ↓ ← →) are used to move the cursor. You can use the cursor arrow keys to move across existing text without changing the text. On most computers, pressing the key marked Num Lock first will produce the numbers on the keypad's set of these keys instead of the arrows.

- The Spacebar is used to enter spaces or blank out text.

- The Home, PgUp, End, and PgDn keys are used for special WordPerfect movements.

- The Tab⇆, ⬅Backspace, Ins, and Del keys are used for special functions described later in this book.

Using a Mouse

If you have never used a mouse before, some of the terminology used in this book may seem strange to you. Here's a quick summary of the mouse techniques you need to know.

- **Point:** To move the mouse until the pointer on-screen points to a specified item.

- **Click:** To press and release the left mouse button.

- **Double-click:** To press and release the left mouse button twice in a row, quickly.

- **Drag:** To hold down the left mouse button while you move the mouse.

Practice these techniques in Windows until you become familiar with them; if you use a mouse with WordPerfect for Windows, these skills will be very important.

Understanding Directories

Since you'll be storing your WordPerfect for Windows files in directories, you should understand what a directory is. A disk can be divided into parts called *directories*. Directories are especially useful on hard disks; they keep certain types of files separate so that you can find what you need easily.

Directories take on the structure of an upside-down *tree*. The first level is called the *root*, and is represented by a backslash (\). Off the root, typically, is a directory for your operating system, along with a directory for each of your applications. In the following diagram, the operating system is DOS, and the applications installed are WordPerfect 6.0 for Windows (WPWIN60) and Windows (WINDOWS). There are also several directories underneath the one for WordPerfect 6.0 for Windows, including one called WPDOCS. That directory is used to store your document files.

C:

    DOS

    WINDOWS

    WPWIN60

        GRAPHICS

        LEARN MACROS

        TEMPLATE

        WPDOCS

        WPDRAW

NOTE: Chapter 13 in this book explains how to use WordPerfect for Windows to create directories, and how to copy documents between directories.

When you use WordPerfect for Windows, you may be asked to enter the *path*, which indicates how to get from where you are to the desired directory. For example, this is the path to a WordPerfect for Windows document called MYDOC.WPD:

C:\WPWIN60\WPDOCS\MYDOC.WPD

First, **C:** identifies the drive. Then, a backslash (\) identifies the root. **WPWIN60** shows the directory for WordPerfect for Windows. Next, **WPDOCS** shows the directory for your Word-Perfect for Windows documents. The name of the document follows. The directory and document names are always separated by a backslash.

Installing WordPerfect for Windows

Before you can use WordPerfect for Windows for the first time, you must prepare the program to run on your computer. This is called *installing*, because a working copy of the program is placed on your hard disk during the procedure. Installing is a one-time operation; once WordPerfect for Windows is available on your hard disk, you can use it again and again.

Because the folks at WordPerfect have you—the first-time user—in mind, the installation process is almost entirely automated. You need to know only some basic information about the type of computer you are using, and how to use your keyboard to respond to the screens WordPerfect shows you.

TIP: During installation, you will be given the option of network installation. Installing WordPerfect on a network is usually considered a fairly advanced task. WordPerfect walks you through installing the *server*, the primary computer with the hard disk to which other computers are attached. It also helps you install the computers, called *workstations*, that are hooked to the server. If you run into problems when you install, don't hesitate to seek help from your dealer, or call WordPerfect technical support.

Starting the Installation

To begin installing WordPerfect for Windows, start up Windows and place the WordPerfect disk with **Install #1** on the label in drive A (or B) of your computer. From the Windows Program Manager, select File, Run. On the Run dialog box, type in: **A:install** (or **B:install**) and select OK.

A dialog box appears for you to enter registration information. Enter your name and license number, then choose Continue. You're taken to the WordPerfect 6.0 for Windows Installation Type dialog box. Select an installation option based on your needs.

- If you're a beginner, select Standard installation; it's the easiest.

- If you're an advanced user, you may want to select Custom installation; it gives you more control.

- If you want to install WordPerfect on a network, select Network installation. (Check with your network administrator first, though.)

- If you have limited space, select Minimum; it places the minimum number of files on your hard disk.

I'm going to assume that you're choosing Standard Installation; it's the best option for beginning users.

After selecting your Installation type, you are asked to specify a drive. C is your best bet. Then you are walked through a series of screens. WordPerfect for Windows tells you when to replace the disk in the drive with another disk. Note the name of the disk WordPerfect requests, find the disk with that label, and place it in the drive.

Never remove or replace a disk in a drive when the drive light is on, or you might damage the disk.

WordPerfect for Windows explains each feature as you install it, and shows you the progress of the complete installation. If you aren't sure that you want to install a particular feature, go ahead and select Yes to install it. Having features you don't use only takes up some space, but failing to install a feature you want later costs you time, and causes confusion when you have to install that feature alone. Plus, until you understand WordPerfect for Windows, it is difficult to distinguish which features you won't need. So, installing each feature early in your WordPerfect experience can only help you.

When installation is done, you're notified. Information about your installation appears, and you're given final instructions.

Once WordPerfect for Windows is installed, place the original disks from WordPerfect Corporation in a safe, temperate environment. These are your final backup copies, so you don't want anything to happen to them.

What's New in WordPerfect 6.0 for Windows?

In two words . . . WordPerfect 6.0 for Windows is *more* and *better*. Even though the earlier version of WordPerfect for Windows was hard to beat, version 6.0 brings more capability. Plus, those features that were already a familiar part of WordPerfect have been improved. Let's see how.

Power Bar: The Power Bar allows you to make speedy selections of often-used features. Chapter 1 introduces the Power Bar, and Chapter 20 describes how to change your Power Bar.

Button Bars: Button Bars allow you to make quick selections with a click of the mouse. WordPerfect comes with several standard Button Bars, and you can make your own. Chapter 20 covers Button Bars.

Enhanced Menus and Dialog Boxes: WordPerfect for Windows is getting streamlined to help you get at the features you need quickly. As you use the features, you'll see that WordPerfect 6.0 for Windows is just plain easier to use.

Ease of Installation: The installation process has been made easier. You can install right from Windows. When saving documents, WordPerfect for Windows sets up a WPDOCS directory off WPWIN60 (the WordPerfect for Windows directory) as a default. There is no need for the novice user to have to create directories right away. Appendix B covers the details.

New Views: There are new views. You may view a document in Draft, Page, or Two Page mode. You may also Zoom in on a view. (Combined, these features replace the old Print Preview feature.) Chapter 4 covers these options.

Managing Files: Managing Files has been greatly simplified. The special File Manager feature is gone. In its place are all the file management functions you need, right where you need them (such as on the Save As and Open File dialog boxes). You may view documents, use the QuickFinder or Quick List, or choose file options like copying, moving, renaming, deleting, or printing a file. You may also use options to create or remove a directory. Chapter 13 covers how to manage files.

Formatting Options: Some WordPerfect for Windows enhancements seem small, but save a lot of time. Here's an example. Instead of setting up complex graphic settings to create a border around a page or some paragraphs, you may select borders for paragraphs or pages directly. This is just one example of small formatting enhancements in WordPerfect 6.0 for Windows that will make for smoother sailing. Chapter 16 covers how to enter borders. Chapter 5 covers setting margins, and Chapters 6 and 7 cover other formatting options.

Mailing Labels and Envelopes: Instead of guesswork, WordPerfect 6.0 provides features designed just for creating mailing labels and envelopes. Creating envelopes during merges is covered in Chapter 15. More information is in your WordPerfect documentation.

Fonts: WordPerfect comes with fonts. See Chapter 6 for details on how to put them to use.

New Print Features: There are more print options, and output options that make it easier than ever to get the printouts you need. Many of these features are covered in Chapter 7.

Handling Pages: You can now use Secondary Page, Chapter, and Volume page numbering. You can also subdivide a page, easily creating tri-fold brochures or booklets.

Grammar Checking: WordPerfect 6.0 for Windows gives you a grammar checker . . . no, a *sophisticated* grammar checker. Chapter 11 tells you how to get started using Grammatik.

Spelling Enhancements: The speller has been improved. For example, now you can set up automatic replacements for words you typically mistype, or acronyms you use often. You can also set up suggested words for those you commonly overuse. Look at Chapter 11.

Bookmarks and Hypertext: You can set up bookmarks, and then use them with Hypertext to shoot from one document to another, or from one spot within a document to another spot. Macros can be started, as well. Check out Chapter 12.

Macro Editing: Editing macros has been improved with the addition of a Feature Bar. See the what and how in Chapter 14.

Merging and Styles: While both merging and styles will seem very familiar to seasoned users (on the surface, at least), enhancements await. Check them out in Chapters 15 and 17.

Graphics: WordPerfect for Windows is giving you increasingly fine control over graphics, along with new features, such as interesting border and appearance options. Chapter 16 covers the details.

Charts and Drawing: WordPerfect for Windows introduces exciting features for creating charts and drawings. With these new graphics functions, you can add three-dimensional charts to your documents, or insert drawings that incorporate text and free-form shapes.

Index

I

X-Z

Quick Command Reference (Menu and Keystroke)

Function	Menu Selections	Quick Keys
Bold	**Layout, Font, Bold**	`Ctrl`+`B`
Center	**Layout, Justification, Center**	`Ctrl`+`E`
Close a document	**File, Close**	`Ctrl`+`F4`
Columns	**Layout, Columns, Define**	`Alt`+`L`, `C`, `D`
Copy selected text	**Edit, Copy**	`Ctrl`+`C`
Cut selected text	**Edit, Cut**	`Ctrl`+`X`
Display Button Bar	**View, Button Bar**	`Alt`+`V`, `B`
Display Power Bar	**View, Power Bar**	`Alt`+`V`, `O`
Display Ruler Bar	**View, Ruler Bar**	`Alt`+`Shift`+`F3`
Envelope	**Layout, Envelope**	`Alt`+`L`, `V`
Exit WordPerfect	**File, Exit**	`Alt`+`F4`
Export a text file	**File, Save As, Format**	`F3`, `Alt`+`T`
Find text	**Edit, Find**	`F2`
Font	**Layout, Font**	`F9`
Font Size	**Layout, Font, Size**	`F9`, `Alt`+`S`
Full Justify	**Layout, Justification, Full**	`Ctrl`+`J`
Grammar checking	**Tools, Grammatik**	`Alt`+`T`, `G`
Graphic box, create	**Graphics, Figure**	`Alt`+`G`, `F`
Graphic box, edit	**Graphics, Edit Box**	`Shift`+`F11`
Graphic line, edit	**Graphics, Edit Line**	*None*
Graphic line, horizontal, create	**Graphics, Horizontal Line**	`Ctrl`+`F11`
Graphic line, vertical, create	**Graphics, Vertical Line**	`Ctrl`+`Shift`+`F11`
Help	**Help**	`F1`
Import a text file	**File, Open, List Files of Type, All Files**	`Ctrl`+`O`, `Alt`+`L`, All Files

continues

Quick Command Reference (*continued*)

Function	Menu Selections	Quick Keys
Import a spreadsheet	Insert, Spreadsheet/ Database, Import	Alt+I, R, I
Italics	Layout, Font, Italic	Ctrl+I
Left justify	Layout, Justification, Left	Ctrl+L
Margins, set	Layout, Margins	Ctrl+F8
New file	File, New	Ctrl+N
Open a file	File, Open	Ctrl+O
Paste selected text	Edit, Paste	Ctrl+V
Print	File, Print	F5
Replace text	Edit, Replace	Ctrl+F2
Reveal codes	View, Reveal Codes	Alt+F3
Right justify	Layout, Justification, Right	Ctrl+R
Save	File, Save	Ctrl+S
Save As	File, Save As	F3
Select text	Edit, Select	Shift+←, →, ↑, or ↓
Select printer	File, Select Printer	Alt+F, S
Sort a list	Tools, Sort	Alt+F9
Spell checking	Tools, Speller	Alt+T, S
Style, creating	Layout, Styles	Alt+F8
Tabs	Layout, Line, Tab Set	Alt+L, L, T
Table, creating	Table, Create	F12
Template, select	File, Template	Ctrl+T
Undelete	Edit, Undelete	Ctrl+Shift+Z
Underline	Layout, Font, Underline	Ctrl+U
Undo	Edit, Undo	Ctrl+Z